Readers respond to
THE VESTIBULE

"I just had a thirty-two-year-old man, an actor by profession, who died of a brain stem tumor. He was searching all over the literature for some accounts of what it is really like to be dying. I was able to send my last copy of *The Vestibule*, and his mother read it to him ten days prior to his death. It was a great consolation, not only to him, but to his family. I am using your book quite extensively because I have about two hundred workshops on death and dying throughout the country."

—Elisabeth Kübler-Ross, M.D., bestselling author of *Death and Dying*

"Thank you for sending me a copy of your book and for the beautiful inscription. It was most thoughtful of you to bring your book to my attention, and I am indeed very grateful to you."

—Hubert H. Humphrey, United States Senate

(Former Vice President Humphrey died just a few weeks after sending his praise.)

"I cannot express on paper the feelings I felt while reading your book. My father's death left many a question in my mind and a great deal of bitterness in my heart. My mother and I got your book shortly after his death, and I read it immediately, as I hoped to find some answers to my questions and some comfort. May I tell you that I cried through many of the chapters. I found a great deal of comfort and understanding of death. Your book showed me that death is not frightening for the ill person. He welcomes it, after all that he has been through. For me, the subject of death no longer makes me tremble."

—Susan Curran, Staten Island, New York

"Thank you for the beautifully written, timely book. A true labor of love."

—Gloria D. Harper, Evanston, Illinois

Other Books by Jess E. Weiss

The Adam and Eve Fantasy (1985)
Overcoming the Fear of Death and Dying (1991)
  (Braille edition published in 1993)

THE VESTIBULE

EDITED AND WRITTEN
BY

Jess E. Weiss

POCKET BOOKS

New York   London   Toronto   Sydney   Tokyo   Singapore

POCKET BOOKS, a division of Simon & Schuster Inc.
1230 Avenue of the Americas, New York, NY 10020

ISBN: 0-671-00417-4

First Pocket Books trade paperback printing March 1997

10 9 8 7 6 5 4 3 2 1

POCKET and colophon are registered trademarks of
Simon & Schuster Inc.

Cover design by Matt Galemmo
Front cover photo by Sally Gall/Gamma Liaison
Text design by Stanley S. Drate/Folio Graphics Co. Inc.

Printed in the U.S.A.

ACKNOWLEDGMENTS

We are grateful for the permission to reprint the following by the publishers and the authors and for the courtesy that they have shown us. The acknowledgments below are greatly appreciated. Much care has gone into tracing the correct sources of ownership. If any accidental errors have occurred, correction will be made in future editions upon notification to the publisher.

"The Atlanta Crash," from *Rickenbacker: an Autobiography.* Copyright 1967 by Edward V. Rickenbacker. Published by Prentice-Hall, Inc., Englewood Cliffs, New Jersey.

"When the Curtains of Death Parted." Copyright 1972 by Martin C. Sampson, M.D. By permission of the author.

"The Window of Heaven." Copyright October 1963 by Julia Phillips Ruopp. By permission of *Guideposts* magazine, by Guideposts Associates, Inc., Carmel, New York.

"I Watched Myself Die." Copyright May 1964 by E. L. Huffine. By permission of *Guideposts* magazine, by Guideposts Associates, Inc., Carmel, New York.

"The Experience of Death" by Dr. Elisabeth K. Ross. By permission of the author.

"Heaven and Hell," from *Heaven and Hell* by Emanuel Swedenborg. By permission of Swedenborg Foundation, Inc., 139 East 23rd Street, New York, New York.

"Return from Tomorrow." Copyright June 1963 by George G. Ritchie, Jr., M.D. By permission of the author and *Guideposts* magazine, by Guideposts Associates, Inc., Carmel, New York.

Acknowledgments

Excerpt from *My Religion* by Helen Keller. Copyright 1927. By permission of Swedenborg Foundation, Inc., 139 East 23rd Street, New York, New York.

"How It Feels to Die" by David Snell. Copyright 1967 Life-Time Inc. All Rights Reserved.

"Character-Building Thought Power," *Character-Building Thought Power* by Ralph Waldo Trine. By permission of the publisher, Dodd, Mead & Company, 79 Madison Avenue, New York, New York.

Realization of Oneness by Joel S. Goldsmith. Copyright 1967. By permission of Lyle Stuart, Inc., New York, New York.

Infinite Way Letters 1957—from Chapter "Resurrection." Copyright 1957 by Joel S. Goldsmith. By permission of the publisher, L.N. Fowler & Co. Ltd., 15 New Bridge Street, London, E.C.A.

"Cardiac Arrest Remembered" by Robert L. MacMillan, M.D. and K. W. G. Brown, M.D. By permission of the authors and originally published in The Canadian Medical Association Journal 104:889, 1971.

"The Hereafter," from *And the Scroll Opened* by George M. Lamsa. Copyright 1967 by George M. Lamsa. By permission of Doubleday & Company, Inc.

I DEDICATE THIS BOOK

to

THE FIRST INFANTRY DIVISION

the

BIG

RED

ONE

and

4,325 COMRADES WHO GAVE THEIR LIVES

FOR THEIR COUNTRY IN

WORLD WAR II

THE FIGHTING FIRST DIVISION

No Mission Too Difficult,
No Sacrifice Too Great,
Duty First.

This division, the "Fighting First" or "the Big Red One," is the oldest and probably the best-known infantry division in the United States Army today. In World War II, it was the first to enter Germany and the first to cross the Rhine.

The "First is first" has always been an axiom in the U.S. Army. It was one of eighty-nine divisions that fought the good fight in World War II, earning twenty distinguished Unit Citations, sixteen Congressional Medals of Honor, and 20,752 individual medals. Total days in combat: 443. It has the magic of its name—the Red One: the Fighting First.

Generals knew that the division able to win its objective with the least loss of life would be that division with the most combat experience. This was the First. It was the first to land at Oran in North Africa, November 8, 1942, taking part in the initial fighting. It was the first ashore in the invasion of Sicily, inching its way up cliffs and along tortuous trails and distinguishing itself by smashing the Hermann Goering Division. And it was the first to hit on a beach named Omaha, on June 6, 1944, cracking Hitler's "Europa's Festung," Europe's Fortress. Casualties for the First Division and its attached units on Omaha Beach were in the neighborhood of 3,000 killed, wounded, and missing. Two assaulting regimental combat teams lost about 1,000 men each within the first bloody hour of fighting, but the Division hung on to the beachhead, forced its way inland by sheer determination, destroyed a whole German division that stood in its way, and prompted journalist Ernie Pyle to write later: "Now that it is over, it seems to me a pure miracle that we ever took the beach at all." For their heroism at Omaha, 740 men of a single battalion of the 16th Infantry were awarded the Bronze Star. I was one of them.

The year 1944 determined the outcome of World War II in Europe, and through it all the Big Red One was in the lead. Few of its soldiers served it continuously from Oran in North Africa to the Elbe in Germany—the chances against them were too great. From Kasserine, a lonely pass in the North African hills; and from El Guettar to Tunisia and to Troina, the hill town of Sicily; and then to the rolling, surging sea edging a bloody beach named Omaha, the most strongly fortified section of the coast; through Normandy and the hedgerows, where the sunken roads of France were death traps; to Mons in southern Belgium, where the Big Red One caught up with a new German army trying to escape from the coastal areas of northern France; and on into the concrete pillboxes of the vaunted fortified Siegfried line outside the invincible city of Aachen, the bastion of German nationalism, where the backbone of enemy resistance was forever broken; and again on to the Battle of the Bulge—the First was always first.

General Eisenhower was keenly conscious of the tremendous role played by the First Division in helping him win the first round of the battle for Europe, and of the magnificent fight of the 16th Regiment in spearheading the invasion of Omaha Beach.

One day in early July 1944, he pinned awards for heroism on the chests of twenty-five First Division heroes and said, *"You are one of the finest regiments in our Army. I shall always consider the 16th my Praetorian Guard. I would not have started the invasion without you. . . ."*

History will remember. When all the veterans who fought the battles have long since passed on, there will remain to startle the emotions, quicken the heart, and enlighten the eye the traditions that men live by, the traditions of the fighting First Division: with the blood and brawn and brains of its men it wrote across the ramparts of two continents an American *Iliad*.

CONTENTS

Contents

The purpose and motive of *The Vestibule* is to establish with more certainty that there is an afterlife, thereby alleviating fully, or to a degree, the sting of death.

—JESS E. WEISS

A LETTER FROM A FRIEND

I was reading and evaluating a revised manuscript of a book published in 1972, entitled *The Vestibule*. While reading it for the third time I was mesmerized because this book treated the very core of existence itself—life after death and immortality.

The author, who survived Normandy's Omaha Beach Invasion of D-Day, June 6, 1944, has stared death in the face. In fact his story became international, being featured in many of the prominent newspapers of the world, including France's *Le Monde;* in addition, his story was a feature on NBC-TV's *Now* program with Tom Brokaw and Katie Couric to commemorate the fiftieth anniversary of D-Day, June 1994.

Then I "tripped the light fantastic" between this life and the hereafter because I was recently struck with a debilitating heart attack from which I am recuperating. The riveting truths of *The Vestibule* dominated my heart and mind infinitely more than my condition. Even though the Supreme Being has for now left me in this life, there is within me more of a reaching out toward that vestibule of immortality. Having veritably brushed against angels' wings, I no longer fear death, because what mankind calls death is actually an entrance into God's genuine life.

With an urgency, I implore you to read this book. Why? Because all of us will face the reality of crossing over into the other side. I cannot yet claim to have walked through the brilliant tunnel that leads to heavenly light, but I have at least stepped onto the outer fringes. I, like the author, have eyeballed death, and all apprehension and fear have disappeared.

Whether or not a person considers himself "religious" or adheres to any faith at all, this book will make a vast difference in his life.

———

Joseph S. Johnson, Jr., Author and Editorial Consultant to Jimmy Carter, Astronaut Jim Irwin, and many outstanding public figures, entertainers, politicians, and athletes.

VICTORY WAS ON THE BEACH

June 6 will always be D-Day. World War II lasted 2,191 days, but June 6, 1944, along a strip of the north coast of France, was the greatest, the hardest, the longest day.

England, France, and the United States—everything hung on it. Europe would be liberated from the Germans. This had been, for four long years of the occupation, as sure as judgment. Every color in the flag, every candle in the church, said it was coming—D-Day. But when it was coming, and where, was then the greatest secret on earth. The secret held. The Germans bought the lies they were meant to.

Then in London and everywhere, soldiers were gone from the street. The next thing anyone knew, in the darkness before June 6, an impossible number of ships formed in the channel, and English cottages were buffeted by the greatest roar of planes ever known. And fathers said simply, "This is it." D-Day, that fabulous day of all the prayers and promises, was here and now and happening.

The day before June 6, Hitler still owned Europe.

The day after June 6, five Allied divisions were out of their boats and holding on to ninety miles of coast. It didn't come easily: Two Americans, two British, and one Canadian division paid the butcher's bill. But, before a year was out, Europe would be free. This because of one day, a rare, almost holy day—June 6, 1944—D-Day.

———————————————

Steve Bergin, author, Vietnam veteran, reservist in the Connecticut National Guard and son of a W.W.II veteran.

D-Day
and the Invasion of Normandy

U.S. Army

Normandy American Cemetery
Colleville-sur-Mer, France
Courtesy of The American Battle Monuments Commission; Washington, D.C.

I would rather be in Hell with God
than in Heaven on earth, without Him.

MEISTER ECKHART

PREFACE

The Vestibule, 1972–1997

At first glance, the assault on the beaches of Normandy on D-Day in 1944 and the publication of *The Vestibule* in 1972 have little, if anything, in common. Yet for me, the two are inextricably linked, the cause and effect, if you will, of my compiling this book—the first to solely concern itself with the issue of life after death.

Before World War II, I had believed in God. Yet after experiencing the horrors of war, and overcoming insurmountable odds, I became increasingly agnostic, even atheistic. I could not reconcile what had occurred and what I had seen with my own two eyes on the battlefields of Europe with a benevolent and peaceful God who reigned supreme, and I reasoned that if there ever was a God, surely He is now "dead." My struggle to regain my faith and conviction in God was overwhelming, almost self-destructive. It took a very long time, and countless internal conflicts, before I regained my faith. And the result of my trials with faith, as you will see, was the book *The Vestibule.*

In 1941, I was among the first ranks drafted to serve my country in World War II. As a very young man, my experiences with death were few: I had never seen a corpse, had never attended a funeral, and no family member or close friend of mine had died. Going into battle, I had no thought or fear of death.

By 1943, I was a corporal squad leader with the Second Battalion, Sixteenth Infantry, First Division—"the Big Red One." And it was with this division that, on the early morning of June 6, 1944, I found myself in the middle of the English channel in five- to ten-foot waves, in a small amphibious Landing Craft Tank (LCT) that was launched from the troopship U.S.S. *Samuel Chase.* We were part of the second wave attacking Hitler's "Atlantic Wall," the formidable German defenses of all the Normandy beaches, which, unknown to the attacking Allies, also included the entire German 352nd Artillery Division, as well as their crack Twenty-first Panzer Division.

Heavy naval and air bombardment preceded our assault, which succeeded in knocking out several enemy installations. However, the beaches were still lined with barbed-wire and mines, and the concrete pillbox emplacements, situated at angles that covered the entirety of Omaha Beach laterally from the sea wall, were left unscarred. As we neared the shore, 155mm howitzer shells began to rain on us from above. I could hear crossing bands of intense and accurate machine-gun and mortar fire hitting the waters and the heavy metal hull of the LCT, from stern to bow.

All of the GIs in the LCT, already weighted down with full field packs, gas masks, rifles, bazookas, ammunition, and bulky life preservers, were jammed together on both sides of the jeeps that were lined up in the center of the craft. When the shelling commenced, my battle-scarred combat buddies and I crouched down and hugged the bottom of the LCT, seeking whatever protection its metal hull could provide. Past experience as a squad leader in the African and Sicilian campaigns taught me how to best protect myself from incoming artillery shells. I had even developed a "second-sense," whereby I could intuit where and how close a shell would hit.

But many on our LCT were new recruits who had not yet experienced combat. I knew this because of the way they talked, how they carried their gear, and by the fact that they did not have the Big Red One shoulder-patch insignia. To these recruits, the shelling sounded like the Fourth of July. Several of them even stood up on the jeeps to get a better view of what was happening. Without a thought I screamed to them, "Hit the deck!" But it was too late. German artillery decapitated two of them, and several others were severely wounded. A buddy named Braddock and I gave the wounded what first aid we could.

The amphibious tanks were designed to splash into the water and chug ashore. But under the intense fire, many LCTs dropped their ramps hundreds of yards from the shore, and their tanks sank like lead caskets, their crews drowning before they could swim free. When our ramp came down, we were aground on a sandbar a few hundred yards from shore. A hail of bullets hit the surf right in front of the lowered ramp. There already were hundreds of GIs struggling in life preservers and on rafts to keep from drowning in the rough waters, and some were attempting to dive underwater to escape the deadly machine-gun fire. Weighted down with full field gear, we were temporary floating targets.

When we hit the water's edge, I saw the bodies of GIs from the first wave hanging lifeless on the barbed-wire iron-crossed stanchions that extended for miles in either direction. Hundreds of other bodies floated facedown, only their knapsacks visible above the bloody waters. Some of us attempted to drag the dead and the wounded to shore. When I hit the beach I lay immobilized, seasick, and exhausted for some time, alongside the dead and decapitated bodies of members of my company for whatever camouflage they could afford.

As I lay frozen amid the pile of corpses, thoughts raced through my mind: *Am I dreaming? Am I dead? What does being dead feel like?* The stern voice of my captain broke my train of thought as he yelled out commands. "Two kinds of people are staying on this beach—the dead and those who are going to die. . . . Now let's get the hell out of here!" I stood up and, to my surprise, my legs moved.

And at ten A.M., on June 6, 1944, the enemy position on the cliff overlooking the beach was finally overrun by the Second Battalion, Sixteenth Infantry. The greatest number of casualties on D-Day were suffered on this bloody Omaha Beach, with one company losing ninety-six percent of its men within fifteen minutes of landing.

In the ensuing campaigns throughout France, Belgium, and into Germany, I witnessed countless dismembered bodies, the decaying flesh of adults and children, male and female, and animal decimation beyond human comprehension. So many times I felt numb and sick with the thought that I was never going to survive the horrors of war. I was going to die on foreign soil, alone, away from loved ones. Despite the fact that I had escaped death so many times in Africa, Sicily, and had even overcome the ungodly odds on D-Day, I grew despondent about dying. Thoughts of ending up in a thick black plastic burial bag, like so many of my buddies, plagued me so much that death became my mortal enemy. Replacement turnover was hourly, and I was one of the few remaining regulars from my original cadre still alive. I even began to pray to be wounded, so that I could end this living nightmare.

It was while defending a captured concrete pillbox on

the Siegfried line outside of Aachen, Germany, that my "prayers" were answered. A German high-velocity mortar shell hit mere inches from my right foot. I heard it coming. I froze. I could not move; I had given up hope and faith, and I was tired of living. Yet I survived, and was subsequently hospitalized for over a year, paralyzed on one side with loss of use of my right arm and a multiple shrapnel hip wound that shortened my right leg. Seventeen pieces of shrapnel still remain in my body today. I was given a service-connected medical discharge and finally sent home.

While I was in the army hospital, after my third unsuccessful operation, the army surgeon told me, "Son, there is nothing more we can do for you. You best go home and make the best of it. Your disabilities are permanent—learn to live with them." From that moment on, I consciously tried to eradicate from my memory the dehumanization, death and inhumanity I had witnessed. It didn't work. When an individual faces death as often as a front-line combat soldier, death and dying become constant traveling companions. Like a camera containing undeveloped film, the conscious mind retains the negative aspects of past experiences, which are ready to be developed at a moment's notice. Nightly I awoke in cold sweats, screaming and struggling to avoid being blown to bits, vividly remembering the faces of those who perished not inches away. Planes flying overhead often prompted me to cower under the bed before I even realized what I was doing. Once, on a train to Washington, pebbles scattered by a train speeding by us in the opposite direction hit my window with a loud rat-a-tat-tat, simulating machine-gun fire. I was embarrassed to find myself crawling to take cover under the seat. Another time, as I was on the way to work, a motorcyclist wearing a German W.W.II helmet sped by the car. Without a thought, I mentally cocked an invisible rifle, raised it to my shoulder, sighted . . . and fired.

This tremendous mental and spiritual burden had even made me apathetic to the fact that, according to the United States Army, I was a war hero. I was decorated with a Silver Service Star and Arrowhead for participation in five major battle campaigns and the assault landing on Sicily in July 1943, the Bronze Star with Oak Leaf Cluster for heroism on D-Day, a Purple Heart, the New York State Conspicuous Service Medal, the Combat Infantryman Badge, Expert Rifleman Badge, and numerous other medals and citations. But the sense of guilt that so many others had died, both by my hand and by others', the fact that I had used their dead bodies for cover so that I might live, and all the atrocious sights, sounds, and experiences of war that remained with me, no matter how I tried to block them from my memory, caused me to reject all of the honors given to me, and to begin a desperate search for answers.

The fact that I had killed in order not to be killed did not sit well with me, and my firsthand experience of man's inhumanity to other men left me emotionally and spiritually devastated. Before the war, I understood my relationship with God, and felt destined for union with Him. But I returned a different man, a lost soul, alone, "crying in the wilderness." Questions filled my head: *Is this mortal life all there is, and if so, what is its meaning? Is there a better life beyond this? Where is God in all of this suffering and death? Does He even exist, or is He now dead? Is He mortal or immortal? Does He exist before birth . . . or in the hereafter? Does death serve a higher meaning?*

My religious beliefs were shaken to the core, and the fear of death overshadowed my new life. Every day became a matter of survival. I struggled to have faith in a God that would be close to me in times of hopelessness and in times of helplessness, a celestial guardian beside me when I lay dying. I needed to know if immortality exists, not in the hereafter, but in the "here" and "now," or I felt I would die. I had even written my own obituary two years after the war. I strove to get in touch with the infinite, but I could not find answers anywhere I looked. All faiths, Eastern and Western, agree that life continues beyond the grave, and one must spiritually prepare for this journey. But how could I when I could not even bear to look at images of Jesus, tortured and in agony on the cross? But, as is often the case in life, man's personal hell leads him to God's heavenly purpose.

In the 1950s, I discovered a row of secondhand bookstores on Second Avenue in New York City. I spent many of my lunch hours in these stores, fascinated by all of the literature on metaphysics, spiritual life, and mystical theology. I began to find great comfort and wisdom in my reading, and my faith was gradually restored by my realization that God was not dead, but rather alive and within reach of anyone who strove toward His light. This gave me hope in overcoming the nightmares of yesterday, the physical and mental handicaps of today, and the fear of death and dying that shadowed tomorrow. I realized that if ever I were to be free—free of the fear of death, of the horror caused by man's hatred, of the burdens of war memories and of my own handicap—I must strive to personally know God, intimately and intuitively.

I began to listen to spiritual and metaphysical tapes in my sleep to overcome the nightmares, and made my own interpretive notes concerning the dreams I had had during the night on a pad I kept by my bedside. This helped me rise above the daily, and nightly, mental miasma of the war. It took me over a decade to get over my negative outlook of my physical handicap, which I also attribute to these spiritually motivating teachings. But overcoming my depression and self-destructiveness was a far greater struggle. Although I was happily married with two children, and successfully self-employed, something seemed to be lacking in my life, something that kept me from enjoying life to its fullest potential. I was not content with just the loaves and fishes. I hungered to know what lay in store for me, if there was some meaning to life, if there was indeed life after death.

In 1968, while studying and meditating, I randomly opened the Bible to a passage by the apostle Paul in his Letter to the Hebrews: "Deliver them who through fear of death were all their lifetimes subject to bondage." As I pondered this profound message, an urge to delve for a deeper understanding of why we fear death inspired me to write about it. But fear again held me back, as I reasoned, "I'm just an insurance agent. What do I know about writing." And I completely forgot about the incident.

A few days later, though, I had the occasion to consult a metaphysician, one who helps patients to learn about the ultimate nature of existence and one's relationship to God. Her office was on the top floor of a high-rise building overlooking 42nd Street and Fifth Avenue in New York. As I was leaving, I glanced out her office windows, and my eyes fixated on the New York Public Library, with its concrete statues of the two majestic lions. A voice suddenly instructed me from within. "Go to the library," it said. I don't know why, but I obeyed, and soon found myself at the library's information desk. I did not know what to say to the attendant, so I sheepishly asked, "Sir, do you know anything about the Bible?" He apologized and said he did not. I then replied, "There's a certain story in the Bible about a man named Lazarus. He died and was entombed in a grave for four days. Then he was brought back to life. Now, my interest is in the four days he spent in limbo. I need to know what he was thinking while he was in that 'dead to the world' state of consciousness."

The man's eyes suddenly lit up, and he pulled a *Life* magazine from a nearby shelf. He opened it and showed me a story about a staff writer who was allergic to penicillin and who was mistakenly given an overdose of the antibiotic and pronounced dead in an ambulance en route to the hospital. He was, however, miraculously resuscitated—brought back to life.

From that moment on, similar personal stories of people who had crossed the threshold into death and had then returned to talk of their near-death experiences somehow found their way to me from various sources. Thus inspired, I began to write for the first time about my post-war reflections on coping with death and dying. Through prayer and meditation, I could finally let loose the emotion and pain I had been blocking out of my mind for so long. My writings made my sense of existence bearable under the most difficult situations. Ideas began to flow within me, and I felt impoverished at times when I was unable to think and write on such subjects as immortality, eternality, and infinite beings. Human existence had purpose for the first time, and I began to see God's divine plan in everything around me.

It was then that I decided that the world needed to know these life-after-death stories. In the late 1960s, the subject of life after death was not a popular discussion topic, superseded by notions of "how to die with dignity." Those who had experienced near-death experiences were reluctant to talk about the phenomenon, and those who did were considered touched in the head. Yet the similarities among the out-of-body narratives that I had found made me realize that mind and body exist separately, and that all I really am is consciousness. I awoke to the realization that my human concept of body is mortal, but my "I am" consciousness is immortal. And that this immortal soul-consciousness is intimately connected with God, with no beginning and no end—a never-ending cycle, untouched by death.

The Vestibule was one of the first books of its kind, and has been used the world over to provide comfort for those who have doubted the existence of God and the potential of the immortal soul. It has put people in touch with their own immortal-selves and helped them cope with the difficulties and trials of earth-life. In addition to answering the most difficult questions—such as "Is there life beyond the grave? Is immortality a reality?"—it has provided comfort and a healing message to terminally ill patients and their families everywhere.

And it is with this mission that *The Vestibule* arrives at its twenty-fifth anniversary. My own personal journey toward enlightenment came full circle upon the fiftieth anniversary of D-Day in 1994, when I, along with thousands of fellow soldiers, returned to the beaches of Normandy. To return is to find things not as they were. The battle images of 1944 had, for the most part, vanished. The beaches of anguish and death are now pristine, breeze-swept and quiet. The terrifying obstacles, the battered hulks of landing craft, the floating bodies, and the burned-out tanks are long since gone. Only the burnt husks of the concrete pillboxes still remain intact.

I was deeply honored to stand at the spot on Omaha Beach where many had given their lives for the ideals we hold so dear in this world, and to grieve at the sight of the

memorials, tributes, and graves of so many of our loved
ones. My story was picked up by NBC, and it featured a
tearful reunion with my foxhole buddy, a man I had not
seen or heard from since the war. (I had previously written an article entitled "Staff Sgt. Herbert Siegel Where
Are You?" for The Battle of Normandy Foundation's
Beachhead Journal in 1993, which helped lead to our reunion.) Like a phoenix risen from the ashes, my greatest
spiritual awakening occurred on the site of my greatest
torment as I realized that those who had fallen and those
who survived, those who despaired from the inhumanity
and cruelty of war and those whose lives were gloriously
uplifted by it, were all part of the triumph of the immortal
spirit, bathed in God's love and presence. "Think not only
upon their passing, remember the glory of their spirit."

Today I can attest that life after death is a fundamental
truth of man's God-like infinite nature, and that man has
to realize this truth and consciously lay hold on to eternal
life. The reissue and revision of *The Vestibule* twenty-five
years after its initial publication in 1972 brings again to
light . . . *there is Life after Death.*

—JESS WEISS
December 1996

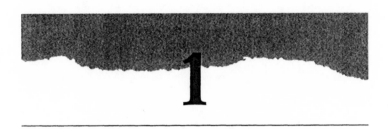

"THE ATLANTA CRASH"

(From *Rickenbacker: An Autobiography*)

Edward V. Rickenbacker

HEAVEN
Is oneness with God-Eternal life;

HELL
Is earthly separation from God

AND
The difference between is measured by
the degree that we fear death and dying.

—Jess E. Weiss

T he Mexico Flyer was a DC-3 sleeper equipped with berths. It had a little private room behind the cockpit called the "sky lounge," and I made myself comfortable there with my paperwork. Over Spartanburg, South Carolina, the pilot came through the doorway from the cockpit.

"Captain Rickenbacker," he said, "the weather in Atlanta isn't too good. We may have some difficulty getting in."

The captain, James A. Perry, Jr., of Atlanta, was a fine young man with an excellent record. Having the boss on board was bound to have some psychological effect on him, and I immediately assured him that he was in command and should do whatever he thought best. That was my standard policy.

The plane continued on toward Atlanta. It was a smooth and even flight. I was sitting by the window. The flight steward, Clarence Moore, was next to me in the aisle seat. We passed through scattered showers, but occasionally the clouds thinned out. I recognized the lights of the Atlanta Federal Penitentiary as we flew over it.

The field reported a low ceiling, and we were making an instrument approach. According to this procedure, we would follow the radio beam in over the airport, fly past it, make a 180-degree turn, and come back on the beam.

I had come into Atlanta on many another cloudy night, and this time everything seemed routine. I felt the pilot put his left wing down to go into the 180-degree turn. There was no way for me to know, and obviously the captain didn't know either, that we were about one thousand feet too low. We shall never know why. Either the field had given him the wrong altitude when he was coming in, or the copilot had misunderstood.

Suddenly I felt the left wing scrape the treetops. The captain felt it simultaneously, for he instantly yanked the left wing up and put the right wing down. I jumped from my seat and began moving swiftly toward the tail of the plane.

Everything seemed to go. I was in the aisle when the right wing hooked into the trees. The wing was ripped off. The plane veered to the right and went up on its nose. I resolved that, if the plane started burning, I would open my mouth and suck in the flames. It's quicker that way.

The lights went off as the pilot cut the switch. I was bouncing around inside and came down on the arm of a seat so hard that my left hip was smashed completely. The plane kept turning over in a somersault. It landed on its tail and broke in two pieces in the middle. I was right where the break occurred. That's where I found myself when the tearing noises stopped—wedged tight in the wreckage. I was lying on the body of Clarence Moore. He was dead.

My head was held tight between the bulkhead and a gas tank. Something had dented my skull. Along the temple over my left eye was a groove you could lay your little finger in. I had a big egg on my forehead.

Wreckage had packed in around my left arm, shattering the elbow and crushing the nerve. The arm was clamped tight. My left hand stuck out of the wreckage, but I couldn't move it at all; it was paralyzed and terribly painful. Later I found that several of my ribs were broken, some in two or three places. Two jagged ends had broken out through my sides. In addition to the crushed hip socket on the left side, my pelvis was broken on both sides. A nerve in my left hip was severed, and my left knee was broken. I couldn't move my body or my entire left leg at all. My right hip and leg were pinned too, but they were not broken. The only part of my body that actually had any movement was my right hand and forearm.

I was soaking wet with a combination of blood and high-octane gasoline. The tanks had ruptured, and gasoline was everywhere. I remembered how the lights had gone out just before the crash. The last action of the pilot and copilot, both of whom were killed instantly, must have been to cut off the ignition to prevent an explosion. At least those of us who were still alive were saved from burning to death.

I began to hear talking around me in the dark. Of the sixteen people on board, eleven were still alive at that time. Some were seriously injured, but others seemed only shaken and dazed. They were the people who had been in the tail. Some were in nightclothes. One man was wandering around in his underwear.

A woman was moaning. There were groans and cries of pain. The rain was falling, and it was cold and wet.

A man's voice said, "Hey, let's start a bonfire and get warm."

"No!" Fear wrenched the word out of me. With hundreds of gallons of 100-octane gasoline soaking everything, we'd all have gone up like a torch.

"Don't light a match," I shouted. The ends of my broken ribs grated painfully against one another as I cried out. "You'll set the gasoline on fire. For God's sake, don't light a match!"

There was silence for a moment. "Who is that?" somebody asked.

"Rickenbacker," I said. "Don't light a match. Just sit tight and wait. Somebody will come and get us."

In the meantime, I was in agony. Of all my injuries, my

left hand was the most painful. I felt for it with my right hand, took hold of the ends of my fingers and yanked as hard as I could. I was desperate enough to try anything. It did relieve the pain slightly, but I didn't have the strength to continue.

In addition to the pain, being so completely immobilized was frustrating and exasperating. Lying on the steward's dead body added to my mental discomfort. In a frenzy, I tried with all my strength to wrench my head loose. It moved a few inches, just enough to make contact with a jagged piece of metal that was sticking out just above my left eye and that I did not see in the dark. It ripped my eyelid, right in the center, and my eyeball popped out of the socket and fell down on my cheek.

But I still wanted to get myself loose. I struggled again, this time with my shoulders and chest. Several ribs snapped. I heard them give. It sounded like popcorn popping.

There were two other passengers trapped in the wreckage near me. From their groans, they seemed to be in even worse shape than I was. I tried to comfort them as best I could. I kept reassuring them that help was coming. I told them that I was sorry on behalf of the airline. Thinking of ways to comfort and control them kept my own mind active. But comfort alone could not keep them alive, and they both slipped off during the night. Now there were seven dead, nine living.

Three of the passengers, all men, had escaped major injury. If they could find a house or a road, it would definitely hasten our rescue. On the other hand, it would be easy for anyone to get lost stumbling around in the hilly pine country on that black and rainy night. I solved this dilemma by instructing one of the men to proceed out from the wreck as far as he could and still remain within the range of my voice. When he had reached that point, I sent a second man out past him along the same projected line to the point where he could barely hear the first man's voice. The third man repeated the procedure.

Though this line extended several hundred feet from the wrecked plane, it was not enough to reach any sign of civilization. Keeping their distances, they then swung around the wreck like a pair of dividers. One of the men fell into a deep ravine in the dark. He wasn't hurt, but he lost some enthusiasm for exploring.

While this human line of communications extended on one side of the crash, I heard voices from the other side. A rescue party was approaching. I shouted back as loud as I could, but nobody heard me. The party went on by, and the voices dwindled in the distance. At first this near-miss seemed tragic. But then I realized that if they had stumbled across the gasoline-soaked wreckage with their kerosene lanterns, they might have set us all on fire.

Finally, in the cold, gray light of early dawn, at about seven, a searching party found us. It took them an hour to cut and pry and loosen the twisted metal that held me. They pulled me out, and I saw myself looking at a camera. Suddenly both camera and photographer disappeared. One of the Eastern boys had pushed the photographer aside, not too gently. Covered with blood and with my eye hanging down on my cheek, I was not very photogenic.

The doctor in the searching party gave me a shot of morphine. It had no effect at all on the pain I was suffering. Dope makes me wilder than a March hare, but the pain was so terrible that I asked for another shot. He gave it to me, and it produced some slight relief.

Members of the searching party guided those who could walk to the road and carried the rest on stretchers. When it came my turn, four men started carrying me to the road. The terrain was rough and the ground was slippery, and every step hurt. Going down the steep side of a ravine, some of my bearers slipped. The stretcher buckled on my broken back and it was all I could do to keep from crying out with pain.

They carried me on across a little creek and finally reached the road. An ambulance was waiting, but the dead were placed on first. The first ambulance drove off filled with corpses. I asked why. Someone said that state law authorized a $20 fee for transporting a dead body but only $10 for a living one.

It was almost an hour before another ambulance arrived and we were loaded aboard. An Eastern pilot who had been in the searching party rode in the ambulance with me. I must have been a horrible-looking mess, with my eye out of its socket, my face black and blue, and the rest of me caked with blood. The pilot suddenly became nauseated from looking at me.

In spite of my condition I couldn't help commenting, "Why are you sick?" I asked. "I'm the one who's supposed to be sick."

I was perfectly rational. I felt every bump on the way to town. Our destination was Piedmont Hospital. Years before, I had anticipated the possibility of accidents and had made arrangements with hospitals all along the route to provide emergency service when and if it should be needed. In Atlanta, Piedmont had been chosen.

At the hospital the attendants rolled me into the emergency room. There were only two interns on duty at that hour to care for nine injured passengers. At that point I was too weak to talk, but I knew everything that was going on. One of the interns took a quick look at me and told the attendants to push me out of the way.

"He's more dead than alive," I heard him say. "Let's take care of the live ones."

I was lying there helpless and speechless when a Catholic priest entered the emergency room. I overheard him ask the nurse my religion. If I were a Catholic, of course, he would give me the last rites. The nurse came over and asked me what I was. Suddenly my voice came back.

"I'm a damn Protestant just like ninety percent of the people," I said.

It was not a tactful remark, even under the influence of dope, but it brought results. The head surgeon of the hospital, Doctor Floyd W. McRae, had been called from his home, and he arrived and took over. It was not the first time Doctor McRae had worked on me. He had assisted in my mastoid operation in Paris in 1918.

First he pushed my eyeball back into its socket; then he sewed up the eyelid to keep it there. He didn't want to use an anesthetic, he told me, as it would affect the muscles of my eye and make the replacement more difficult. To hold me still, one of the interns put both hands on my shoulders and pushed down hard. I heard my broken ribs go snap, crackle, and pop, and I let out a bellow of profane protest.

Doctor McRae calmly went ahead and finished sewing up the eyelid. I have had good vision in my left eye ever since; it's better than my right one. The crash actually improved my nose. It had been a little off center, thanks to being broken six times in my life. That time, the seventh, left it perfectly straight.

A full complement of doctors had arrived at the hospital to take care of the injured passengers. Doctor McRae had me rolled into the operating room, where members of his staff and a couple of outside specialists looked me over. They all began arguing about what they could do.

I could tell from the way the surgeons talked that they were all, in their minds, busily sharpening up their scalpels. I was half out of my head with the effects of the dope, and one of the doctors wanted to bore a hole in my skull at the indentation to relieve the pressure.

They also discussed my smashed hips and broken pelvis. The ball of the joint had crushed the socket and ridden up on top of it. My left leg was four inches shorter than my right. There was much discussion of whether they should operate on the hip, set it, or leave it alone. Then I heard the calm assured voice of Floyd McRae.

"Well, gentlemen," he said, "we may let him die on our hands, but we will never kill him."

I popped off again. "Nuts!" I said. "Get me a good osteopath, and I'll be out of this place in three days."

There was no operation.

Adelaide happened to be visiting with friends in Charlotte, North Carolina, at the time. The boys were in school in Asheville, not too far away. The three hastened to Atlanta. Ralph Greene, Eastern's medical chief, came up from Miami and stayed by my bedside day and night.

The next morning Doctor McRae suggested I be given a little brandy. Brandy was the last thing I wanted, but they mixed up a little in a milk shake and fed it to me anyway. It must have worked, because right away I realized that I was starving.

"Wouldn't you like something else?" Doctor McRae asked.

"You bet I would," I said. "I want a bottle of beer and a ham-and-egg sandwich."

By that time the doc knew better than to argue with me. He sent out for a ham-and-egg sandwich and a bottle of beer. It was a delicious meal.

The lobby of the hospital was crawling with reporters.

"The Atlanta Crash"

When Ralph McGill, editor of the *Atlanta Constitution*, called to ask how I was, the doctor told him that I was getting a lot better.

"Why, he just asked for a ham-and-egg sandwich and a Coca-Cola," he added.

That story went out all over the world. The Coca-Cola Company, which has its headquarters in Atlanta, sent up one of their largest coolers to be installed in my room, and it was kept loaded with Cokes.

On Saturday it was decided to put me in a plaster cast in order to let the bones start knitting. "Eddie," Doctor McRae said, "we're going to have to wrap you up. It's going to be painful, as we can't give you an anesthetic."

"Go ahead," I said. "I can take it."

He was right. They had to turn me over as they put on the wet, plaster-impregnated bandages, and the pain was excruciating. But I took it. When they were through, I was in plaster from my chin to my toenails. Only one of my arms was free. A contraption was rigged up over the bed to hold my legs up at an angle, so that the blood would not settle in my feet.

By Sunday morning, I seemed to have improved. Doctor McRae called Adelaide, and they decided that the boys could go back to school. They left about eight in the morning on the bus.

Two hours later, I suddenly took a turn for the worse. I began to die. I felt the presence of death. I knew that I was going. The sensation was the same as that when I had nearly bled to death following the tonsillectomy back in 1917.

You may have heard that dying is unpleasant, but don't you believe it. Dying is the sweetest, tenderest, most sensuous sensation I have ever experienced. Death comes disguised as a sympathetic friend. All was serene; all was calm. How wonderful it would be simply to float out of this world. It is easy to die. You have to fight to live.

Doctor McRae could see that I was going. He called Adelaide at her hotel and told her to hurry over. She called the state police and told them to intercept the bus that the boys were on and bring them back to their dying father's bedside. The patrol car, with David and Bill in it, hit 80 and 90 miles an hour. The boys loved it, they admitted later.

The troopers had to stop for gas on the outskirts of Atlanta. They told the attendant to hurry up because they were taking Eddie Rickenbacker's boys to his bedside.

"Well, you don't need to hurry anymore," the fellow said. "He died an hour ago. News just came over the radio."

Fortunately, the news was exaggerated, and the troopers brought the boys in so that they could see for themselves.

When they came into the room, I was having an hallucination brought on by the morphine. I thought that I saw the most delicious-looking cherries and grapes hanging from the bar over my head. I asked the boys to pick some of that luscious fruit. David, the older boy, understood that I was not myself, but Bill took me seriously.

"But, Daddy," he said, "I don't see any grapes or cherries." He turned to Adelaide and said, "Mother, is Daddy always going to be nuts like that?"

But that was only a brief moment of comic relief in what was the greatest fight of my life—and for my life.

Because I had decided not to die. I recognized that wonderful mellow sensation for what it was, death, and I fought it. I fought death mentally, pushing away the rosy sweet blandishments and actually welcoming back the pain.

*And this is the will of Him that sent me,
that everyone which seeth the Son, and
believeth in Him, may have everlasting life. . . .*

—John 6:40

I t was in August of 1957. My mother had just left the boat, a fifty-foot twin-engine Matthews cruiser, to pick up Dad at the train station. We had been charging batteries for about seven or eight hours. I had just gone down to the engine room to get a screwdriver when a violent explosion went off. Violent enough to break a whole series of windows within a three-quarter-mile radius of Cold Spring Harbor. The brute force of the explosion hurled the exhaust manifold, which weighed over three hundred pounds, a good quarter of a mile across the bay.

My body shot up several feet through the mahogany overhead, and dropped back down, landing between the two engines. I noticed that gas was running out of the gas lines and the thought came, "Boy, this is about to go off again."

I rushed to the stern of the boat, where we had a little dinghy with an outboard motor. How I ever reached it I will never know, for I was as black as a charred marshmallow, with second- and third-degree burns over eighty percent of my body. The only parts of me that were not burned were the cheeks of my fanny, the soles of my feet, and my privates.

As I attempted to start the motor of the dinghy, the skin of my hands came off like arm-length gloves. The flash heat had cracked all the flesh and the pulp that was there, and in trying to start the engine, the rope cut right through the tendons. The dinghy would not start. Fortunately, help soon came from a runabout which pulled alongside of the boat, and as we pulled away, I noted, I had left the skins of my hands on the back of the outboard. Later, someone tried to sell the flesh to my wife thinking she might want to use it to make a lamp shade. Reminiscent of the Nazi Auschwitz horror days!

When we got to the dock, the ambulance had not yet arrived, but the firemen were there. We could not wait. They could not even put a blanket over me, so they rushed me to the emergency room of Huntington Hospital, where I remember scaring a nurse half to death.

It was amazing that I was so coherent all through this experience. I have my preparatory training to thank for that. I went through Admiral Farragut Training Academy in anticipation of attending Annapolis or the United States Merchant Marine Academy at Kings Point, New York. Later, I had pre-med training at Rollins College in Winter Park, Florida, and I was also qualified to be a Boeing 707 pilot for a large airline. I truly believe that all the instruction and preparation I had received prior to the accident enabled me to be indifferent and rational under this severe test.

I was well aware of the seriousness of my situation and requested immediately that my wife, Doris, be contacted; also a close friend, Dr. William Holt. I wanted to get my affairs and insurance matters in order. But, most important, I wanted Bill Holt to evaluate the medical problem for me because I was not getting any straight answers from the hospital staff. Bill came out and his first remark was, "You damn fool."

I loved the guy because he would always shoot straight from the shoulder. My reply was, "Alright, Bill, how long am I going to be conscious and how long have I got to live?"

"Not more than twenty-four hours, maybe forty-eight at the most." Then the curtain came down. "Burris," he said, "the odds are ninety-nine to one against you."

Bluntly I replied, "Bill, take care of my wife and help her on the insurance, and make damn sure they don't short-change me on the Demerol and morphine because I do not want to go for any pain."

Bill Holt is one of the truly great men I have known. He was a famous obstetrician and cardiologist. Three days later he appeared at my bedside with Doctor Beverly Chew Smith, one of the head surgeons from Roosevelt Hospital in New York. Bill was pleased that I was still alive. They learned that I was headed for surgery at nine-thirty the following morning. They were going to amputate both arms and both legs. They told me this, and added, "We don't think you will survive the operation."

Bill said, "It is unethical for me to come in and announce this to you, but if we could take you to Roosevelt Hospital, we think we could save your hands, and maybe your legs, too. Dr. Littler is over at Bellevue and he is the world's greatest burn expert. I think we can get him to guide us in handling this case."

So I submitted to the debridement at Roosevelt. It took about four and one half hours and from seven to nine doctors, with Doctor Littler overseeing the whole operation.

Days later, to pass the time I was watching TV, although I was not particularly interested in the program. Then the commercial came on. A moment later I was looking back at a patient in the very hospital bed in which I had been. The patient tried to identify himself as me. I shuddered away from the thought and ignored it. Slowly I circled the room backwards, always going backwards through this whole experience, and always going faster and faster without control or direction. I went through the fourth-floor window and into the hospital courtyard above New York City and above the clouds. All the time

THE VESTIBULE

I was rationalizing, "Better make a mental note of that courtyard," because this was not just hallucination. It had absolute reality to it. I knew the difference. I wasn't able to speak. There didn't seem to be a need for it. There was no sensation of warmth or cold, just complete comfort. There was, however, always this great sense of acceleration through intergalactic space, the curvature of the earth, the clouds, the whole astronaut's view. [Editor's note: This experience preceded by several years the astronauts' first space flight.]

As I passed the orbit of the moon, suddenly I realized I had passed through the Solar System itself. My passing view was the earth, several planets, the sun, the Milky Way, and the edge of the galaxy. As the acceleration increased, the density of the stars began to become less and less. Even the galaxy appeared as a star itself. It was at this point that I first became concerned. The idea of death entered my thoughts: "Maybe you are dead because time does not seem to be a factor and this could go on forever."

Certainly I was traveling faster than the speed of light, because I recall making a mental note of "who says you can't go faster than the speed of light—you're doing it now."

Suddenly, I remembered my wife would have to catch up with me, but no, she couldn't, because she is slower than I am. Well, maybe I could catch up with someone ahead. Then it dawned on me, no, I wouldn't be able to because they would be going faster than me.

The revelation came that it is possible to be totally alone for eternity. Time is part of limitless space; there is just no limit to how far you can go. At this point, my concern was: Who was I going to catch up with? Who was I going to leave behind? Would I be totally isolated for eternity? This sense of absolute loneliness scared me. In this terrified state, I became aware of countless beings, friendly like myself, who communicated. They were in great harmony with a light that was off to my right and all around me. (Remember, I am still traveling backwards.) This light is indescribable; it is a light that generates everywhere, yet it is not a light like our sunlight or anything like it. It is Living Light and all these beings are in harmony and in communication with it. I thought, "This must be God—the Ultimate Being," only I am not with It. I can't talk to It, communicate with It, and It isn't talking to me.

Then I sensed that I was not going to be one of those harmonious beings and would revolve eternally alone. If it is possible for the soul to scream, I screamed, "God help me!"

That fast I was back in bed watching the same television commercial. It had ended. The first thing I did when I was able to get out of bed was to run over to the window to take a look at the courtyard. It was "right on target"—it looked exactly the same as when I went out the window, for I had never seen it before, having been rolled into the hospital on a stretcher as an emergency patient.

Several weeks later I left the hospital. This experience shook me considerably and I hollered for answers from every preacher around, figuring that this was their realm and they could give me some insight. None of them had any answers. Up to this point in my life, I had considered myself an atheist. I just did not believe in God.

This experience started me thinking about religion and I knew then that someday I would get into the service of this Being. I suspected it would probably be through Christ. I really had no recognition of who or what Christ was. I became a believer in God at this point. Periodically, the event would come to consciousness and I would pass it by with the thought that someday I'd do something about it. Whenever a discussion about God came up, I would impress others with, "How could you possibly believe there is no God?" I would then relate my experience affirming that such a thing could not have happened without God.

In 1962, I was transferred to Military Air Transport Service, Moffat Field, Japan.

One day I was to meet Doris, my wife, to go to the movies. The movie theater was just two parking lots directly across the field from our squadron. It was nightfall and the street light lamps lit up only the walks. The parking lots were in complete darkness. As I sauntered along, across the lots, the thought came to my mind, "I think I will go into the Christian Ministry." Suddenly as though someone turned on a light switch in a darkened room, I found myself immersed in a great light that seemed to say "yes" and that seemed to penetrate my entire being. It was through, above, and around me, and most important, I was part of it. I had experienced this light once before, only I had ignored It then, even though I was alone traveling through and around It, I was not with It nor was I a part of It.

Later in my life, when I read of Paul's happenings on the road to Damascus, I realized the similarity of the experience, but I was not physically affected, as Paul was.

I began to attend church regularly and became vitally interested in the Christian faith. I finally came to recognize Christ, who He really is. It was something that I had to wrestle with for quite some time. I requested to be allowed to leave the military service. The Vietnam War was starting up.

I had all the good fitness reports, a golden Navy career, a promotion within the year, and a guaranteed retirement within a few more years. Everybody said, "Burris, you're crazy for going out of the Navy. What are you going to do it for?" I told my closest friend, "I want to go into the ministry." His reply was, "You've gone around the bend." One gorgeous day while flying down to Okinawa, on our way to Clark Field in the Philippines, the clouds and the Pacific were just as blue as they could be. It couldn't be more beautiful. Sitting there in the cockpit I thought, "You crazy guy, what are you going to leave all this for? To kick over a golden career and everything that goes with it. What are you going to do about your family? How are you going to support them? Where is the money going to come from? You're thirty-seven years old, and coming up on forty and this is not something to take lightly." And I didn't know what to do. But once you've heard the call, you've heard the answer.

In earlier days, Jim Hayes, a dear friend, had said to me, "Once having stood in the glory of God only a fool would walk away."

I couldn't deny the call. Naturally, I wondered whether I was a fool or not. When we arrived in Okinawa, I went into a bookstore that I had frequented hundreds of times during six years of flying in the Pacific. The crew went to eat, but I stopped in for something to read instead. Normally, this bookstore contained anywhere from five hundred to a thousand books. Yet this day there were only eight or ten copies of one book. The remainder of the shelves lay empty. The book was *A Man Called Peter* by Kathryn Marshall. Well, I was nicknamed "Big Bert the Crusher" by my squadron, and it just wouldn't do to see Big Bert reading a religious book by Kathryn Marshall, so I quietly stuffed the book into my back pocket.

I went back to the airplane, took off, and put the copilot in the pilot seat, and the navigator in the cockpit, and went back to the navigation station and opened the book. It seemed to just open itself to the Matthew passage, "Seek ye first the Kingdom of God and his righteousness; and all these things shall be added unto you." The answer to all my worries and doubts about material things came to me right at that portion of the Sermon on the Mount. Then I read the rest of Peter Marshall's life, and my whole life since has been based on that one clause, "SEEK YE FIRST." I can assure you that the results are unbelievably wonderful.

Reverend Jenkins, who was a minister on Long Island, is now retired and living in upstate New York.

3

WHEN THE CURTAINS OF DEATH PARTED

Martin C. Sampson, M.D.

There is no death, what we call death
  Is but a sudden change;
Because we know not where it leads,
  Therefore it seemeth strange.
There is no death, what we call death
  Is but a restful sleep;
They wake not soon who slumber so,
  Therefore we mourn, we weep.
There is no death, what we call death
  Is but surcease from strife;
They do not die whom we call dead,
  They go from life—to life.

—Anonymous

I t was a hot Philadelphia summer day, and the air in the old Pennsylvania Hospital hung heavy and still. I had been up all night in a vain fight to save a little girl from meningitis. In reaction to her death I was feeling completely disheartened. As a young intern I had seen so much dying in the past months that life seemed fragile and meaningless. I was face to face with cynicism. Faith seemed to exist only to be mocked by death.

The first patient I was to examine that morning was a man I shall call John Bradley. He was in his late forties, with deep-set brown eyes and a gentle face. During the few weeks since his admission his condition had declined steadily. As I looked through the window of his oxygen tent I saw that his lips were blue, his breath fast and strained. I knew that his heart had been weakened by rheumatic fever in his youth, and that in recent years hardening of the arteries had taxed it even more.

I couldn't help thinking of his wife, a small, white-haired woman with a face in which the shadows of work and sorrow mingled with faith and trust. She and her husband had constantly looked to me for help. Why, I thought bitterly, did they ask so much of me?

I went over Bradley's medications again in my mind, hoping to think of something new to relieve his suffering. He was getting digitalis to control his failing heart, an anticoagulant to prevent the formation of clots in its damaged wall, and injections to help rid his body of excessive water. The amount of oxygen being pumped into his tent had been increased. That day, I inserted a needle to draw off any fluid that had accumulated in his chest. Still, when

I left him I had the feeling that all my efforts were fruit-less.

Shortly after six o'clock that evening the nurse in charge of Bradley's ward called me to come at once. I reached his bed within seconds, but already his skin was ashen, his lips purple, and his eyes glazed. The pounding of his heart could be seen through the chest wall, and the sound of his breath was like air bubbling through water.

"One ampoule of lanatoside C and start rotating tourni-quets, quickly," I said to the nurse.

Intravenous lanatoside C would give the rapid action of digitalis. The tourniquets would keep the blood in his legs from circulating and temporarily relieve the failing heart—but only temporarily.

An hour later Bradley began to breathe more easily. He seemed aware of his surroundings and whispered, "Please call my family."

"I will," I said.

He closed his eyes. I was just leaving when I heard a deep gasp. I wheeled and saw that he had stopped breath-ing. I put my stethoscope to his chest. The heart was beat-ing, but faintly. His eyes clouded over, and after a second or two his heart stopped.

For a moment I stood there, stunned. Death had won again. In that moment I remembered the little girl who had died the night before and a wave of fury came over me. I would not let death win again, not now.

I pushed the oxygen tent out of the way and started arti-ficial respiration, meanwhile asking the nurse for Adren-alin.

When she returned, I plunged the syringe full of Adren-alin into the heart. Then I whipped the needle out and listened through my stethoscope again. There was no sound. Once more I started artificial respiration, frantically trying to time the rhythm of my arm to twenty strokes a minute. My shoulders were aching and sweat was running down my face.

"It's no use," a flat voice said. It was the medical resident, my senior. "When a heart as bad as this one stops, nothing will start it again. I'll notify the family."

I knew he had the wisdom of experience, but I had the determination born of bitterness. I was desperately resolved to pull Bradley back through the curtains of death. I kept up the slow rhythmic compression of his chest until it seemed so automatic it was as if a force other than myself had taken over.

Suddenly there was a gasp, then another! For a moment my own heart seemed to stop. Then the gasps became more frequent. "Put the stethoscope in my ears," I said to the nurse, "and hold it to his chest." I kept pumping as I listened. There was a faint heartbeat!

"Oxygen!" I called triumphantly.

Gradually the gasps lengthened into shallow breaths. In a few minutes Bradley's breathing grew stronger, and so did his heartbeat.

Just then the screen around the bed was moved slightly, and Mrs. Bradley stood beside me. She was pale and frightened. "They told me to come right away!"

Before I could answer, Bradley's eyelids quivered. "Helen," he murmured.

She touched his forehead and whispered, "Rest, John, dear—rest."

But he struggled for speech. "Helen, I told them to call you. I knew I was going. I wanted to say good-bye."

His wife bit her lip, unable to speak.

"I wasn't afraid," he went on painfully. "I just wanted to tell you—" he paused, his breathing heavier, "—to tell you that I have faith we'll meet again—afterward."

His wife held his hand to her lips, her tears falling on his fingers. "I have faith, too," she whispered.

Bradley smiled faintly and closed his eyes, a look of peace on his face.

I stood there, filled with a mixture of exhaustion, wonder, and excitement. The mystery of death was right in this room. Could I, in some way, begin to understand it? I leaned forward and very softly asked, "John, do you remember how you felt? Do you remember seeing or hearing anything just now, while you were—unconscious?"

He looked at me for a long moment before he spoke. "Yes, I remember," he said. "My pain was gone, and I couldn't feel my body. I heard the most peaceful music." He paused, coughed several times, then went on: "The most peaceful music. God was there and I was floating away. The music was all around me. I knew I was dead, but I wasn't afraid. Then the music stopped, and you were leaning over me."

"John, have you ever had a dream like that before?"

There was a long, unbearable moment; then he said, with chilling conviction, "It wasn't a dream."

His eyes closed and his breathing grew heavier.

I asked the ward nurse to check his pulse and respiration every fifteen minutes, and to notify me in case of any change. Then I made my way to the interns' quarters, fell across my bed, and was instantly asleep. The next thing I heard was the ringing of the telephone beside my bed.

"Mr. Bradley has stopped breathing. There's no pulse."

One glimpse of his face told me that death had won this time.

Why, then, had the curtains of death parted briefly to give this patient another few minutes on earth? Was that extra moment of life the result of chance chemical factors in his body? Or did it have a deeper, spiritual meaning?

Had his spirit been strong enough to find its way back from death just long enough to give a message of faith and farewell to his wife? Could it also have been meant to give a small glimpse of eternity to a troubled and cynical young intern?

Whatever the meaning, and whether or not it had a purpose, the incident made a deep impression on me. This was my first step toward acceptance of certain mysteries as an essential part of life. This acceptance, the gift of a dying patient whom I could not save, put me on the road back to faith.

4

"THE WINDOW OF HEAVEN"

Julia Phillips Ruopp

Never the spirit was born;
the spirit shall cease to
be never.

Never was time it was not;
End and beginning are dreams!

—Bhagavad-Gita

dow of heaven was a flash of revelation about the meaning of life itself.

Now I watch eagerly as each new day brings its lessons
and its blessings, and I am at peace with the belief—no,
the conviction—that in the sight of God the world we live
in and the world of my vision are really one.

5

THE EXPERIENCE
OF DEATH

Elisabeth Kübler-Ross, M.D.

What is it to cease breathing,
but to free the breath from its
restless tides, that it may rise
and expand and seek God unencumbered?

—Kahlil Gibran

When I was a little girl in Switzerland, my mother often told us stories from her own childhood. One of these stories related to the death of her great-grandmother, who lived in the same small village where most of her relatives resided. As it was—and still is—the custom there, the deceased was laid out in her Sunday-best clothes, a church book under her chin, to be visited by friends and relatives paying their final respects prior to the burial in the village cemetery.

Her great-grandmother had been a difficult and determined woman, and many a visitor spoke openly and freely about her—not always in complimentary terms. On the day of the burial after most visitors had left to get dressed up for the gathering, my mother, at the time a small girl, returned once more to say good-bye to her great-grandmother alone. As she tiptoed to kiss her good-bye, she noticed that the old woman's chin moved, making the little churchbook fall. The church bells were already ringing when she ran out of the room notifying everybody that her great-grandmother was not dead but alive.

The old woman lived for another eight years after her presumed death. During those years the only person she spoke to was my mother, who remembered her as being very quiet and serene after this close experience with death. She often told my mother that *death* was a peaceful existence but *dying* was something that people were afraid of.

Seventy years later, I recalled my mother's childhood memory when my work with terminally ill patients brought back those early recollections. I had often wondered why my patients were so afraid of dying and felt somewhat sorry that we had no means to find out what it was really like. Why did so few of my patients really fight death at the end? Why did so few of them die in a state of rage and anger? Why did so many of them have this indescribable expression of utter peace on their faces, similar to the Unknown of the Seine? What did these patients experience when their physical existence ceased to be?

In my workshops on Death and Dying we interviewed over five hundred terminally ill patients. A few of them had come close to dying in Intensive Care Units, as a result of drowning, car accidents, or injuries during the war. Many of them related experiencing a feeling of peace and calm after they were able to overcome the initial fear, shock, or pain of the injury. Drowning victims often related a "passing of memories, faces of loved ones, and important incidents appearing in a kaleidoscopic fashion." The final conscious awareness was always described as a rather pleasant experience. This was also true of suicidal patients who had used either an overdose of drugs or gas (carbon monoxide) and then were rescued in time to tell about their experiences.

In a recent newspaper publication similar experiences are related by patients and their physicians. Five reputable physicians describe the phenomenon of life after death and tell of experiences of some of their patients who unexpectedly had a "comeback." One patient, who was declared dead after inhalation of fumes from a leaky gas pipe, recalled later that her late mother had appeared, smiled at her, and communicated to her that everything was fine. *"At that moment all my fears vanished,"* the patient said.

Another man in his mid-forties, who was pronounced

dead after a massive heart attack, recalled floating toward a passageway and approaching a bright light and voices. Then the gates went further and further away in spite of his wish that they stay. When he woke up, seeing his wife and children, he understood why the gates had receded, but he added, "When my time comes to die I will die willingly."

In an attempt to gather more data about the questions of Life and Death we questioned as many patients as possible to shed light into this unknown area. Mrs. S. was the only patient among five hundred whom we truly considered to have died, from the standpoint of present medical knowledge.

She was a patient in her fifties with a twenty-year history of Hodgkin's disease, and had been hospitalized on many occasions. She had been introduced to me earlier by another terminally ill patient as the "woman who cannot die." We spent many hours talking to each other and she volunteered to attend one of our seminars for members of the helping profession. At these seminars we asked patients to be our teachers and to share with us what it is like to be seriously ill. One of the reasons for her reputation as one who "cannot die" was the fact that she had been in the Intensive Care Unit in several hospitals, often critically ill, and somehow had always come out of it able to resume her role as a housewife and mother. Her only unfinished business "on this earth" (as she put it) was providing for her fifteen-year-old son who had not been well cared for during her many hospitalizations. Her husband, although schizophrenic, had been a fairly good man. When he became psychotic, however, he became very abusive toward the boy and often beat him without provocation. Mrs. S. was able to make arrangements for her son's placement with relatives after his sixteenth birthday. The patient was convinced that she could "hold out that long" and "everything would be all right after that."

She was discharged from the hospital about six months prior to the son's birthday and readmitted five months later. It was during this last stay on the ward that she called me and requested to be invited again to the seminar for nurses, students, and clergy.

With the group she shared her long history of illness, her pride in living a useful life in spite of it, and her final concern for her youngest son. It was almost the end of the class when I asked her why she had been so insistent on talking to us a second time. It was only then that she was able to reveal something to us that she had never mentioned before: About a year earlier, she had been hospitalized in a local hospital for internal bleeding problems. She recalled lying in her hospital room alone, getting weaker and weaker. She contemplated whether she should call for a nurse for help, or "let go." At this moment a nurse entered her room, took one look at her, and ran out. Mrs. S.'s next recollection was of the arrival of a resuscitation team and their working on her revival. She was able to give minute details of who entered her room, how they reacted, and what they were doing on her body while she herself floated a few feet above, observing the procedure performed on her body. Asked how she had felt at that time, she said that she only had one desire, and that was to convey to the physicians and nurses to relax, to let go, not to be so upset. She somehow also knew that she would not be able to communicate her feelings of peace and acceptance to them. She then floated away— unaware that the team gave up their efforts to revive her.

She came back to consciousness as an orderly wheeled her body toward the morgue and she lifted the bedsheet off her face. For understandable reasons, no one desired to discuss the incident with her. When she was physically well enough to be released from the hospital, she was discharged without any discussion of this certainly unusual and traumatic incident.

I asked her if this was the reason why she used our seminar to bring this out in the open. She admitted that she had to talk to somebody about it, but her main question was one regarding her own sanity. She insisted on knowing whether I would regard her as psychotic if I were to label this phenomenon. Without a moment's hesitation I denied this. I realized only later that she was afraid to share this experience with someone out of a concern that if she were labeled "psychotic" (like her husband), her last will concerning the care of her son after her death would be made invalid.

Mrs. S. was grateful for our acceptance and relieved that we did not have a need to give this phenomenon a label. We acknowledged in her presence that there were many things we still did not know about Life and Death and that shared experiences like hers would ultimately shed some more light and understanding into this area. She thanked us profusely and returned to her ward. She was discharged shortly afterward. We were informed of her death a few weeks later, a few days after her son's sixteenth birthday.

Needless to say, the medical students, clergy, and nurses had a vivid discussion, expressing disbelief, shock, anger, or admiration for this woman whose important message to us all seemed to be: "Don't be afraid, it is a feeling of utmost peace when you die." Many students were uncomfortable to terminate the discussion without giving this experience a label of "depersonalization," "hallucination," "delusion," etc.

Mrs. S. had one aspect in common with most of our patients who had accepted their finiteness and who had a second lease on life: She was no longer afraid to die; she lived life fuller and enjoyed it more day after day than some people do in a lifetime. She did not become more religious in a "churchy" sense of the word, but she did impress me as a deeply religious person, who appreciated life and loved people with a new intensity unknown to her prior to this close experience with death.

This is just one more reason why we hope that combined efforts of parents, teachers, schools, and churches can help the people in our death-denying society to relearn to accept birth and death as part of life rather than to shy away from it with fear and incomprehension.

———————

Dr. Elisabeth Kübler-Ross is widely renowned as the world's foremost expert on the subjects of death, dying, and the afterlife, having worked with dying patients of all ages for over two decades.

6

"HEAVEN AND HELL"

Emanuel Swedenborg

HEAVEN

*God. Without whom
there is no heaven.*

HELL

Life without God.

—Jess E. Weiss

After death, man is possessed of every sense, and of all the memory, thought, and affection, that he had in the world, leaving nothing behind except his earthly body.

It has been proven to me by manifold experience that when man passes from the natural world into the spiritual, as he does when he dies, he carries with him all his possessions, that is, everything that belongs to him as a man, except his earthly body. For when man enters the spiritual world or the life after death, he is in a body as he was in the world, with no apparent difference. But his body is then spiritual, and thus separated or purified from all that is earthly; and when what is spiritual touches or sees what is spiritual, it is just the same as when what is natural touches or sees what is natural. So when a man has become a spirit he does not know otherwise than that he is in the same body he had in the world and thus does not know that he has died.

Moreover, a man's spirit enjoys every sense, both outer and inner, that he enjoyed in the world: he sees as before; he hears and speaks as before; smells and tastes; and when touched, he feels the touch as before; he also longs, desires, craves, thinks, reflects, is stirred, loves, wills, as before; and one who takes delight in studies, reads and writes as before. In a word, when a man passes from one life into the other or from one world into another, it is like passing from one place into another carrying with him all things that he had possessed in himself as a man; so that by death, which is only the death of the earthly body, man cannot be said to have lost anything really his own.

Furthermore, he carries with him his natural memory, retaining everything that he has heard, seen, read, learned, or thought in the world from earliest infancy even to the end of life, although the natural objects that are contained in the memory, since they cannot be reproduced in the spiritual world, are quiescent, just as they are when one is not thinking of them. Nevertheless, they are reproduced when the Lord so wills. But more will be said presently about this memory and its state after death. A sensual man finds it impossible to believe that such is the state of man after death, because he cannot comprehend it; for a sensual man must think naturally even about spiritual things; therefore anything that does not appeal to his senses; that is, that he does not see with his bodily eyes and touch with his hands (as is said of Thomas, John 20: 25, 27, 29) he denies the existence of.

The first state of man after death resembles his state in the world, for he is then likewise in externals, having a like face, like speech, and a like disposition, thus a like moral and civil life; and in consequence he is made aware that he is not still in the world only by giving attention to what he encounters, and from his having been told by the angels when he was resuscitated that he had become a spirit. Thus is one life continued into the other, and death is merely transition.

The state of man's spirit that immediately follows his life in the world being such, he is then recognized by his friends and by those he had known in the world; for this is something that spirits perceive not only from one's face and speech but also from the sphere of his life when they draw near. Whenever anyone in the other life thinks about another he brings his face before him in thought, and at the same time many things of his life; and when he does this, the other becomes present, as if he had been

sent for or called. This i:
thoughts there are sha
there as in the natural v

So all, as soon as the
nized by their friends,
way known to them; an
afterward associate in a
in the world. I have ofter
from the world were
again, and that their fr
they had come. Very co
together and congratula
gether, and this for a lor
their delight in living tog

Emanuel Swedenborg (1
losopher, and author, wh
divine revelation that led
founder of a religious se
America.

7

RETURN FROM TOMORROW

George G. Ritchie, Jr., M.D.

I show you a mystery.
We shall not all sleep,
but we shall all be changed.

—I Cor. 15:51

When I was sent to the base hospital at Camp Barkeley, Texas, early in December, 1943, I had no idea I was seriously ill. I'd just completed basic training, and my only thought was to get on the train to Richmond, Virginia, to enter medical school as part of the Army's doctor-training program. It was an un-heard-of break for a private, and I wasn't going to let a chest cold cheat me out of it.

But days passed and I didn't get better. It was December 19 before I was moved to the recuperation wing, where a jeep was to pick me up at four A.M. the following morning to drive me to the railroad station.

A few more hours and I'd make it! Then about nine P.M. I began to run a fever. I went to the ward boy and begged some aspirin. Despite the aspirin, my head throbbed, and I'd cough into the pillow to smother the sounds. Three A.M.—I decided to get up and dress.

The next half-hour is a blur to me. I remember being too weak to finish dressing. I remember a nurse coming to the room, and then a doctor, and then a bell-clanging ambulance ride to the X-ray building. Could I stand, the captain was asking, long enough to get one picture? I struggled unsteadily to my feet.

The whir of the machine is the last thing I remember.

When I opened my eyes, I was lying in a little room I had never seen before. A tiny light burned in a nearby lamp. For a while I lay there, trying to recall where I was. All of a sudden I sat bolt upright. The train! I'd miss the train!

Now I know that what I am about to describe will sound incredible. I do not understand it any more than I ask you to; all that I can do is relate the events of that night as they occurred. I sprang out of bed and looked around the room for my uniform. Not on the bedrail; I stopped, staring. Someone was lying in the bed I had just left.

I stepped closer in the dim light, then drew back. He was dead. The slack jaw, the gray skin were awful. Then I saw the ring. On his left hand was the Phi Gamma Delta fraternity ring I had worn for two years.

I ran into the hall, eager to escape the mystery of that room. Richmond, that was the all-important thing— getting to Richmond. I started down the hall for the outside door.

"Look out!" I shouted to an orderly bearing down on me. He seemed not to hear, and a second later he had passed the very spot where I stood as though I had not been there.

It was too strange to think about. I reached the door, went through, and found myself in the darkness outside, speeding toward Richmond. Running? Flying? I only know that the dark earth was slipping past while other thoughts occupied my mind, terrifying and unaccountable ones. The orderly had not seen me. What if the people at medical school could not see me either?

In utter confusion I stopped by a telephone pole in a town by a large river and put my hand against the guy wire. At least the wire seemed to be there, but my hand could not make contact with it. One thing was clear: In some unimaginable way I had lost my firmness of flesh, the hand that could grip that wire, the body that other people saw.

I was beginning to know too that the body on that bed was mine, unaccountably separated from me, and that my job was to get back and rejoin it as fast as I could.

Return from Tomorrow

Finding the base and the hospital again was no problem. Indeed I seemed to be back there almost as soon as I thought of it. But where was the little room I had left? So began what must have been one of the strangest searches ever to take place: the search for myself. As I ran from one ward to the next, past room after room of sleeping soldiers, all about my age, I realized how unfamiliar we are with our own faces. Several times I stopped by a sleeping figure that was exactly as I had imagined myself. But the fraternity ring, the Phi Gam ring, was lacking, and I would speed on.

At last I entered a little room with a single dim light. A sheet had been drawn over the figure on the bed, but the arms lay along the blanket. On the left hand was the ring.

I tried to draw back the sheet, but I could not seize it. And now that I had found myself, how could one join two people who were so completely separate? And there standing before this problem, I thought suddenly:

"This is death. This is what we human beings call 'death,' this splitting up of one's self." It was the first time I had connected death with what had happened to me.

In the most despairing moment the little room began to fill with light. I say "light," but there is no word in our language to describe brilliance that intense. I must try to find words, however, because incomprehensible as the experience was to my intellect, it has affected every moment of my life since then.

The light which entered that room was Christ; I knew because a thought was put deep within me, "You are in the presence of the Son of God." I have called Him "light," but I could also have said "love," for that room was flooded, pierced, illuminated, by the most total compassion I have ever felt. It was a presence so comforting, so joyous and all-satisfying, that I wanted to lose myself forever in the wonder of it.

But something else was present in that room. With the presence of Christ (simultaneously, though I must tell it one by one) every single episode of my entire life had also entered. There they were, every event and thought and conversation, as palpable as a series of pictures. There was no first or last, each one was contemporary, each one asked a single question, "What did you do with your time on earth?"

I looked anxiously among the scenes before me: school, home, scouting, and the cross-country track team—a fairly typical boyhood—yet in the light of that presence it seemed a trivial and irrelevant existence.

I searched my mind for good deeds.

"Did you tell anyone about Me?" came the question.

"I didn't have time to do much," I answered. "I was planning to, then this happened. I'm too young to die!"

"No one—" the thought was inexpressibly gentle "—is too young to die."

And now a new wave of light spread through the room already so incredibly bright, and suddenly we were in another world. Or rather, I suddenly perceived all around us a very different world occupying the same space. I followed Christ through ordinary streets and countrysides, and everywhere I saw this other existence strangely superimposed on our familiar world.

It was thronged with people. People with the unhappiest faces I ever have seen. Each grief seemed different. I saw businessmen walking the corridors of the places where they had worked, trying vainly to get someone to listen to them. I saw a mother following a sixty-year-old man, her son I guessed, cautioning him, instructing him. He did not seem to be listening.

Return from Tomorrow

Suddenly I was remembering myself, that very night, caring about nothing but getting to Richmond. Was it the same for these people; had their hearts and minds been all concerned with earthly things, and now, having lost earth, were they still fixed hopelessly here? I wondered if this was hell. To care most when you are most powerless; this would be hell indeed.

I was permitted to look at two more worlds that night—I cannot say "spirit worlds" for they were too real, too solid. Both were introduced the same way; a new quality of light, a new openness of vision, and suddenly it was apparent what had been there all along. The second world, like that of the first, occupied this very surface of the earth, but it was a vastly different realm. Here was no absorption with earthly things, but—for want of a better word to sum it up—with truth.

I saw sculptors and philosophers here, composers and inventors. There were universities and great libraries and scientific laboratories that surpass the wildest inventions of science fiction.

Of the final world I had only a glimpse. Now we no longer seemed to be on earth, but immensely far away, out of all relation to it. And there, still at a great distance, I saw a city, but a city, if such a thing is conceivable, constructed out of light. At that time I had not read the Book of Revelation, nor, incidentally, anything on the subject of life after death. But here was a city in which the walls, houses, streets, seemed to give off light; while moving among them were beings as blindingly bright as the One who stood beside me. This was only a moment's vision, for the next instant the walls of the little room closed around me, the dazzling light faded, and a strange sleep stole over me. . . .

To this day, I cannot fully fathom why I was chosen to

75

return to life. All I know is that when I woke up in the hospital bed in that little room, in the familiar world where I'd spent all my life, it was not a homecoming. The cry in my heart that moment has been the cry of my life ever since: Christ, show me Yourself again.

It was weeks before I was well enough to leave the hospital and all that time one thought obsessed me: to get a look at my chart. At last the room was left unattended; there it was in terse medical shorthand: Pvt. George Ritchie, died December 20, 1943, double lobar pneumonia.

Later, I talked to the doctor who had signed the report. He told me that there was no doubt in his mind that I had been dead when he examined me, but that nine minutes later the soldier who had been assigned to prepare me for the morgue had come running to him to ask him to give me a shot of Adrenalin. The doctor gave me a hypo of Adrenalin directly into the heart muscle, all the while disbelieving what his own eyes were seeing. My return to life, he told me, without brain damage or other lasting effect, was the most baffling circumstance of his career.

Today, over twenty years later, I feel that I know why I had the chance to return to this life. It was to become a physician so that I could learn about man and then serve God. And every time that I have been able to serve our God by helping some brokenhearted adult, treating some injured child, or counseling some teenager, then deep within I have felt that He was there beside me again.

Dr. George Ritchie now resides in Kilmanock, VA. This article was published three times in Guidepost *magazine, in the seventies and eighties.*

8

MY RELIGION

Helen Keller

*The best way to get to heaven
is to take it with you.*

—Henry Drummond

I had been sitting quietly in the library for half an hour. I turned to my teacher and said, "Such a strange thing has happened! I have been far away all this time, and I haven't left the room." "What do you mean, Helen?" she asked, surprised. "Why," I cried, "I have been in Athens." Scarcely were the words out of my mouth when a bright, amazing realization seemed to catch my mind and set it ablaze. I perceived the realness of my soul and its sheer independence of all conditions of place and body. It was clear to me that it was because I was a spirit that I had so vividly "seen" and felt a place thousands of miles away. Space was nothing to spirit! In that new consciousness shone the Presence of God, Himself a Spirit everywhere at once, the Creator dwelling in all the universe simultaneously. The fact that my little soul could reach out over continents and seas to Greece, despite a blind, deaf, and stumbling body, sent other exulting emotions rushing over me. I had broken through my limitations and found in touch an eye. I could read the thoughts of wise men—thoughts which had for ages survived their mortal life, and could possess them as part of myself. If this were true, how much more could God, the uncircumscribed Spirit, cancel the harms of nature-accident, pain, destruction, and reach out to his children. Deafness and blindness, then, were of no real account. They were to be relegated to the outer circle of my life. Of course I did not sense any such process with my child-mind; but I did know that I, the real I, could leave the library and visit any place I wanted to, mentally, and I was happy. That was the little seed from which grew my interest in spiritual subjects.

THE VESTIBULE

What is so sweet as to awake from a troubled dream and behold a beloved face smiling upon you? I love to believe that such shall be our awakening from earth to heaven. My faith never wavers that each dear friend I have "lost" is a new link between this world and the happier land beyond the morn. My soul is for the moment bowed down with grief when I cease to feel the touch of their hands or hear a tender word from them; but the light of faith never fades from my sky, and I take heart again, glad that they are free. I cannot understand why anyone should fear death. Life here is more cruel than death. Life divides and estranges, while death, which at heart is life eternal, reunites and reconciles. I believe that when the eyes within my physical eyes shall open upon the world to come, I shall simply be consciously living in the country of my heart. My steadfast thought rises above the treason of my eyes to follow sight beyond all temporal seeing!

Suppose there are a million chances against that one that my loved ones who have gone are alive. What of it? I will take that one chance and risk mistake, rather than let my doubts sadden their souls, and find out afterward. Since there is that one chance of immortality, I will endeavour not to cast a shadow upon the joy of the departed. I sometimes wonder who needs cheer most, the one that gropes on here below, or the one that is perhaps just learning truly to see in God's light. How real is the darkness to one who only guesses in the shadows of earth at an unseen sun! But how well worth the effort it is to keep spiritually in touch with those who have loved us to their last moment upon earth!

Certainly, it is one of our sweetest experiences that when we are touched by some noble affection or pure joy, we remember the dead most tenderly, and feel powerfully drawn to them. And always the consciousness of such a faith has the power to change the face of mortality, make adversity a winning fight, and set up a beacon of encouragement for those whose last support of joy seems taken from them. There is no such thing as "otherworldliness" when we are convinced that heaven is not beyond us, but within us. We are only urged so much the more to act, to love, to hope against hope and resolutely to tinge the darkness about us with the beautiful hues of our indwelling heaven, Here and Now.

I cannot understand the poor faith that fears to look into the eyes of death. Faith that is vulnerable in the presence of death is a frail reed to lean upon. With steadfast thought I follow sight beyond all seeing, until my soul stands up in spiritual light and cries, "Life and death are one."

━━━━━━━━━━━━━━━

Helen Adams Keller (1880–1968): Deaf and blind from age nineteen months, became America's spokesperson, author, and lecturer on behalf of the blind worldwide.

9

"HOW IT FEELS TO DIE"

David Snell

A little more than twenty-four hours ago, as I write this, I learned what it is like to die.

By nearly every clinical standard, an arresting of life did occur. The cause of my "death" was a condition known as anaphylactic shock, induced, in my case, by an acute allergic reaction to penicillin.

For most people, a dosage of this drug, properly administered, is beneficial. For me, with long-dormant allergic factors lurking in my system, the drug could hardly have been more hostile. The allergic onslaught was massive and swift. Had I reached the doctor a minute or two later I could not have survived. A busy phone, a misplaced ignition key, a blocked street—any number of things could have made the difference.

By the rarest combination of good circumstances I was delivered in time into the competent hands of a general practitioner whom I shall simply call the Doctor, in keeping with her own wishes. Slumped in a chair in her office, I was slipping across the honed edge of death. For a period of some minutes there had been no pulse, no blood pressure, no pronounced stirring of the heart. In the last extreme seconds, only awareness remained of the vital functions. As the crisis deepened, I was acutely, almost electrically, aware of things around me and then, when this awareness receded, of things within me. I was an enthralled witness to my own rapidly advancing demise. And at the end I gazed into something that I believe to be life's supreme mystery.

The emergency that confronted the Doctor on that Saturday morning was a meeting of two chains of circumstances. One involved my own medical history; the other involved the Doctor's methodical and intelligent approach to the practice of medicine.

The circumstantial chain on my side began with my first encounter with penicillin some twenty-five years ago. To knock out a strep throat, a doctor gave me an injection of the then-new wonder drug. A few days later I had a mild allergic reaction in the form of hives. The doctor prescribed some pills, the swellings went away, and I forgot all about it. Thereafter, I was given penicillin a number of times—once quite massively, after an appendectomy— with never a discernible ill effect.

The circumstantial chain on my present Doctor's side began with her foresight in assembling a special "setup" of equipment and drugs to cope with emergencies in which decisive and immediate steps must be taken to save a life. Providentially, to this layman at least, she had acquired a vial of Neutrapen—an enzyme which specifically attacks and destroys penicillin—against the day when she might be confronted with penicillin-induced anaphylactic shock. She put the vial into her satchel, along with one containing Adrenalin and another containing a high-potency antihistamine and a special set of sealed hypodermic syringes with which to administer all three. There the Neutrapen remained, in its factory wrappings, its seal unbroken—a tiny unnoticed burden, on countless rounds and house calls—for ten years.

Earlier in the week I had developed a nasal irritation. Saturday morning I awoke with a raw and scratchy throat. I suspected that it might be a strep infection, and made a mental note to give the Doctor a call later on in the day. Then I looked into the medicine cabinet for some throat lozenges and saw the bottle of penicillin tablets left over from a pediatrician's prescription for my children. Why bother the Doctor on her weekend, I thought? Although I was aware that self-prescription is poor business, I took two 250,000-unit tablets—a standard dosage. It was shortly after seven A.M.

During the next half-hour, I went through the morning routine of feeding the dog and brewing coffee. While listening to news broadcasts, I became aware of a prickly sensation on my ankles and legs. It spread rapidly to the wrists and palms, then across the shoulders, lower back, and chest. Suddenly, the itching took fire and I went into a frenzy of scratching. I could see coin-size white blotches rising on the backs of my hands, and then I remembered that long-forgotten penicillin reaction.

I called to my wife, who was still asleep.

"What on earth's the matter?" she asked.

"Hives," I said.

I told her about the penicillin and how a similar thing had happened once before. It still had not dawned on me that the portent was ominous.

"I'd better call the Doctor," my wife said. She had read that a penicillin reaction can be extremely dangerous.

"The Doctor says we must come at once," she said, putting down the phone. "I'll start the car. We've got to hurry!"

Now I was prepared to believe it. I scarcely recognized the swollen, crimson-splashed face that stared back at me from the mirror. The itching was turning to pain and I was experiencing a pronounced asthmatic, choking sensation. Suddenly I was across the bed, one knee on the floor. I realized that I had fainted. I think it was at this point that the thought of real danger crossed my mind and I lurched to my feet.

I remember pausing on the top of the stairs and wondering how I could possibly keep my balance all the way down. In a kind of Mack Sennett slow motion I made it, my legs moving in that high-kneed way of puppets. I wondered who was manipulating the strings. Now the kitchen floated past. In the garage I tried to approach our Volkswagon bus but reeled in the opposite direction. My wife caught up with me as I wobbled onto the driveway, knees starting to buckle. Then I was inside the car, lying on my back across the middle row of seats.

While we drove the seven blocks to her office, the Doctor had put the available minutes to urgent use. Without taking time to dress, she had laid out and activated her setup. She broke the seal of the Neutrapen vial and reconstituted its powdered contents with 2 cc. of sterile water. She loaded three syringes, one with the entire contents of the Neutrapen vial and the others with the Adrenalin and antihistamine. Then she took up her station at the door to await our arrival.

The Volkswagon stopped. As the door spilled open and my wife started tugging me out, I saw a flash of color at the head of the walkway. It was the Doctor in her red-and-blue plaid dressing robe, looking decidedly unprofessional against the backlight of the morning glare. Momentarily rejuvenated by the rest during the car trip, I was able to make it up the walk and into a leather armchair in her office.

Nine minutes had elapsed since my wife's call. I was approximately three minutes away from my confrontation with death.

At a stand to my left the Doctor double-checked her setup. As she did so, she addressed my wife: "Call the police. Ask for an ambulance as quickly as possible." She spoke with quiet authority and no trace of excitement or fluster.

For me, a kind of euphoria was setting in. It was marked by detachment, hyperalertness, and exaggerated good humor. "Now, Doctor," I said as she swabbed alcohol on my left arm, "there's nothing wrong that a good shot of penicillin won't fix."

The Doctor gave no sign that she heard. She was preparing to inject the Adrenalin to start my heart, which now was all but dormant.

From far away, as though on some disembodied arm, I felt the tickle of the hypodermic and a tightening little knot as the solution of Adrenalin flowed into the muscle. And I observed, but thought it curious that I did not feel, that the Doctor was taking my pulse.

When an allergic reaction has set in, a chemical called histamine is excessively generated within the body, causing an increase in the permeability of cells throughout the body. This produces the effects commonly associated with allergy—a rash, an asthmatic swelling of the respiratory passages, or a fit of sneezing. In acute cases, the blood's serum and lymph spill through capillary walls in a floodtide and the blood itself piles up in pools instead of returning to the heart. This is the swift chain-reacting characteristic of anaphylactic shock. Unless the condition can be reversed, the body must die.

To buy a little time by attacking the histamine, the Doctor next sponged my upper right arm and injected the high-potency antihistamine, Chlor-Trimeton.

In a military sense, the injection of Adrenalin and antihistamine had been tactical and defensive. Now it was the time for the all-out assault with the Neutrapen, a mechanism of strategic overkill aimed squarely at the penicillin. It was the weapon with which the war within my system could be won or lost.

Dimly now, for my external awareness was receding, I saw the Doctor probing for a vein in the crook of my left arm. Then the Neutrapen was started on its mission—to seek and destroy the penicillin. Now it was up to the bloodstream to deliver.

But at that moment, the Doctor later said, there was no pulse, no discernible pressure, movement, or flow of blood. The Adrenalin had not taken effect.

Suddenly I knew.

"Am I dying, Doctor? Is it now?" No reply, or rather, none that I could hear.

External awareness had slipped away—I heard, saw nothing. I sagged forward as my wife held my head to keep me from pitching out of the chair. To the Doctor, I had reached clinical death. But for me, there was a surge of internal awareness—magnified, finely focused, brilliant.

It is a progressive thing, this death. You feel the toes going first, then the feet, cell by cell, death churning them like waves washing the sands. Now the legs, the cells winking out. Closer now, and the visibility is better. Hands, arms, abdomen, and chest, each cell flaring into a supernova, then gone. There is order and system in death, as in all that is life. I must try to control the progression, to save the brain for last so that it may know. Now the neck. The lower jaw. The teeth. How strange to feel one's teeth die, one by one, cell igniting cell, galaxies of cells dying in brilliance.

Now, in retrospect, I grope for this other thing. There was something else, something that I felt or experienced or beheld at the very last instant. What was it? I knew it so well when it was there, opening before me, something more beautiful, more gentle, more loving than the mind or imagination of a living creature could ever conceive.

But it is gone.

The thunderclap of Adrenalin into the heart, reverberations through the grottoes and canyons and cliffs and peaks of the body. Sprays of sleet, gale-driven against my nakedness, stinging, slashing. Then blur of motion, sounds of voice.

It is only three or four minutes since I first settled in the leather armchair. The Doctor is at my right side, feeling my pulse as I stir from the coma. Her husband, a surgeon, in his blue dressing robe, has appeared from somewhere and is holding the other pulse. "Well," he is saying, "we're getting a good pulse now. Good and strong."

The ambulance moves, sunlight through the windows, glimpses of trees in chartreuse bud. An oxygen cup is placed over my nose and mouth. I suck hungrily at the odorless nothingness.

Now the bump-bump-bump of potholes, the honk-honk-honk of the ambulance horn as traffic is encountered. Good sounds. Sounds of life and the living.

"No siren?" my wife asks.

"We don't have one," says the woman in white.

Inside the oxygen mask I raise my voice in a wild howl. The woman in white takes alarm, but my wife gets the message. She smiles and blinks back the tears.

"He's supplying the siren," she says.

David Snell's article provided the inspiration and the impetus for the author to begin to compile stories for this book.

10

"CHARACTER-BUILDING THOUGHT POWER"

Ralph Waldo Trine

When love has carried us above all things . . . we receive in peace the Incomprehensible Light, enfolding us and penetrating us. What is this Light, if it be not a contemplation of the Infinite, and an intuition of Eternity? We behold that which we are, and we are that which we behold; because our being, without losing anything of its own personality, is united with the Divine Truth.

—Jan van Ruysbroeck

To me we are here for divine self-realization through experience. We progress in the degree that we manipulate wisely all things that enter into our lives, and that make the sum total of each one's life experience. Let us be brave and strong in the presence of each problem as it presents itself and make the best of all. Let us help the things we can help, and let us be not bothered or crippled by the things we cannot help. The great God of all is watching and manipulating these things most wisely and we need not fear or even have concern regarding them.

To live to our highest in all things that pertain to us, to lend a hand as best we can to all others for this same end, to aid in righting the wrongs that cross our path by means of pointing the wrongdoer to a better way, and thus aiding him in becoming a power for good, to remain in nature always sweet and simple and humble, and therefore strong, to open ourselves fully and to keep ourselves as fit channels for the Divine Power to work through us, to open ourselves, and to keep our faces always to the light, to love all things and to stand in awe or fear of nothing save our own wrong-doing, to recognize the good lying at the heart of all things, waiting for expression all in its own good way and time—this will make our part in life's great and as yet not fully understood play truly glorious, and we need then stand in fear of nothing, life nor death, for death is life. Or rather, it is the quick transition to life in another form; the putting off of the old coat and the putting on of a new; the falling away of the material body and the taking of the soul to itself a new and finer body, better adapted to its needs and surroundings in another world of experience and growth and still greater divine self-realization; a going out with all that it has gained of this nature in this world, but with no possessions material; a passing not from light to darkness, but from light to light; a taking up of life in another form just where we leave it off here; an experience not to be shunned or dreaded or feared, but to be welcomed when it comes in its own good way and time.

The one who takes sufficient time in the quiet mentally to form his ideals, sufficient time to make and to keep continually his conscious connection with the Infinite, with the Divine Life and forces, is the one who is best adapted to the strenuous life. He it is who can go out and deal, with sagacity and power, with whatever issues may arise in the affairs of everyday life. He it is who is building not for the years, but for the centuries; not for time, but for the eternities. And he can go out knowing not whither he goes, knowing that Divine life within him will never fail him, but will lead him on until he beholds the Father, face to face. He is building for the centuries because only that which is the highest, the truest, the noblest, and best will abide the test of the centuries. He is building for eternity because when the transition we call death takes place, life, character, self-mastery, divine self-realization—the only things that the soul when stripped of everything else takes with it—he has in abundance. In life, or when the time of the transition to another form of life comes, he is never afraid, never fearful, because he knows and realizes that behind him, within him, beyond him, is the Infinite wisdom and love; and in this he is eternally centered, and from it he can never be separated. With Whittier he sings:

O God, thou art my God; early will I seek Thee; my soul thirsteth for Thee, my flesh longeth for Thee in a dry and thirsty land, where no water is. . . .

—Psalms 63:1

The other day a lady stopped me as I moved through the crowded aisle of a passenger jet. "Captain," she said, "I just want you to know I'm going to be praying all the while we are in the air."

"Ma'am," I said, "I'll be ahead of you. I start praying while we're still on the ground."

I wish there'd been time to tell her about the prayer I've used at every take-off for twenty-five years, since the time in 1938 when I didn't make it. . . .

My love affair with airplanes started when I was a small boy in Smith Center, Kansas. Out in the field picking cotton I'd occasionally see a plane fly overhead. How I longed to be up there, free as a bird.

The desire to fly grew stronger as I got older and, when at age nineteen I married, my wife, Roselyn, had to live with it too. It was the depression then. My only regular job was with the WPA—still we managed to put something aside each month toward buying a plane. I think I knew Roselyn was saving and scrimping not because she really wanted a plane, but only to make me happy.

But love of planes can be a kind of madness. I fine-combed the aircraft-for-sale columns until I could give the price of any plane for sale anywhere. One day I was startled to find one listed for only $800—half what others were bringing. Excitedly, I showed it to Roselyn.

"But, honey, we don't have $800!" she said.

"Maybe he'll sell for less."

Roselyn walked to the bureau, took out the money we had saved for so long, and gave my hand a little squeeze as she put the bills in it.

At dawn the next morning I was at the airport named

in the ad. Even the lovely sunrise could not hide the fact that there were holes in the fuselage, drooping wings, a flat tire, and a rusted engine. The final touch was a pair of birds flying in and out of their nesting place in the tail.

Despite all this, I bargained with the owner and offered him all I had—$450.

Finally he signed. "Well, okay—take it. It's yours."

When the plane was delivered, a neighbor let me use his pasture to keep it in. At last I had an airplane and an airfield; now all I had to do was learn to fly it. After weeks of patching my plane and running the engine to keep my spirits up, I located a pilot, who gave me three days of lessons. What an unforgettable moment when my plane first lifted off the ground and I was airborne! For the next few weeks my heaven seemed very near as I flew over town and fields, all the familiar landscapes.

At last I felt I could fly well enough to take Roselyn up for her first flight. I helped her into her new helmet and goggles and assisted her into the rear seat of the pusher. I swung the propeller and climbed proudly into the cockpit. A gusty wind was blowing and the temperature was in the high nineties. Better be careful, I thought, the field is short and Roselyn's weight will make a difference in the take-off distance.

I advanced the throttle full open. Almost immediately I knew that we were accelerating slower than usual. Halfway down the field I was still undecided if we could get enough speed to clear the hedgerow at the end of the field. At the three-quarter mark I knew it was too late to stop. I couldn't; there were no brakes. I decided to wait for the last second before trying to pull the plane into the air. Instinctively, I uttered a prayer: "Dear God, we're in

Your hands!" I pulled the ship into the air about forty feet from the hedgerow. The plane shakily rose a bare five feet. It plunged through the hedge, ripping off the wings, and flipped on its back. I was thrown from the cockpit; my head struck the ground.

Now comes the part of the experience which was so strange, and yet so beautiful. With that blow on my head, I was suddenly observing the whole scene from about fifty feet away from the plane. I saw Roselyn struggling to unfasten the safety belt which still held her. Hot vapor burst from the engine. At last Roselyn rolled free onto the ground. There was another form on the ground too. I knew it was mine, but it did not contain the consciousness with which I was observing all that was happening. Roselyn was dragging the body away from the smoking plane, but I watched with indifference.

It was such a profound revelation! I felt myself as clear as light. There was no sense of pain, only a feeling of completeness and well-being.

I saw cars pouring into the field from the highway, people milling about, talking excitedly. I could hear distinctly every word that was said. My attention was particularly drawn to a man and a woman far out at the edge of the crowd.

"Well, he must have been a wild one!" the woman was saying. "It's no more than he deserved! Only birds are supposed to fly!"

An old friend came running onto the field. He pushed through the crowd to Roselyn.

"Is he dead?"

"I don't know, Ed," she sobbed.

Ed stooped down and felt my pulse. "Somebody hurry! Get an ambulance!" He straddled my body and started to apply artificial respiration. There was no response; the body remained inert. Suddenly, Ed grabbed my shoulders, shaking my body violently.

He began to shout over and over: "Roy! Roy! Can you hear me?"

At the sound of my name I felt as if a strong wire was tugging me back toward my body. I was reluctant to return and continued to look on, experiencing the most complete contentment. Ed kept calling my name. The pull became stronger each time he called me, and suddenly I was looking up into their faces.

"Oh my God, Roy, we thought you were gone!" Ed panted. Roselyn was holding my hand, tears streaming down her face.

Ed helped me as I staggered to my feet. I felt a curious drive to get over to the couple who had been talking about me.

"I heard what you said about me," I told the woman.

The woman looked startled; they were standing well out of earshot from where my body had lain. "I didn't say anything."

I repeated what I had heard. She turned ashen and fled to her car.

In my mind's eye, every detail of that experience remains, never dimming. Since then, as an airline captain I have flown over six million miles, carrying hundreds of thousands of passengers. But as the throttles are thrust forward on my giant jet, I always repeat the prayer I said in my pusher so many years ago.

"Lord, we're in Your hands!"

It is not a prayer for protection in the air more than any other place: Flight today seems almost incredibly safe and dependable to those of us who flew the wooden boxes of yesterday. It is more a shout of praise, an affirmation of the truth I discovered one day in a Kansas cow pasture. We are truly in His hands today, and forever. The spirit inside us does not die with accident, disease, or age, but emerges into the closer presence of Him who has upheld us in His grasp from the beginning.

E. L. Huffine last made his home in Englewood, CA.

12

"RESURRECTION"

(From *Infinite Way Letters—1957*)

Joel S. Goldsmith

Everybody who has ever lived from the beginning of all time is still alive—it could not be otherwise. If, however, you catch this vision, when the time comes for you to leave this world, you will step out into a transitional experience which will be higher and better than this one.

—Joel S. Goldsmith
(from *Realization of Oneness*)

I t is said in Scripture that the last enemy that shall be overcome is death. The Master, Christ Jesus, proved this statement by raising the dead. "For I have no pleasure in the death of him that dieth . . . wherefore turn yourselves, and live ye." With such scriptural authority, you should realize that death need be no part of anyone's experience. Acceptance of a process which culminates in passing on is but the acceptance of a universal belief so tenacious that, according to the Master, it is the last enemy that will be overcome. That is probably true. It may take many, many generations before we come to that place in consciousness where we can say with assurance:

I need not die, I, my true identity, my God-identity, can raise up this temple every three years, every three days, every three months. I am continuously renewing this body. I, the Christ of God, the reality of man, am forever about the Father's business of sloughing off, rebirthing, renewing, restoring, and resurrecting this vehicle for my expression.

That I, the Christ, can never be revealed to mortal or material consciousness, but our realization of the Christ uplifts consciousness, until it is so spiritualized that it can behold the inner vision of eternality and immortality here and now.

Let us go back through the years to the resurrection of the Master. Why did only about five hundred people witness the risen Jesus? There were multitudes at the Crucifixion, but only about five hundred witnessed the bodily Resurrection. Why? When Jesus stepped out of the tomb, He walked out of it in the same form in which you and I will walk out of tombs when, to human sense, we seem to pass on. Not one of us will ever remain in a tomb longer than three days, and most of us will never find ourselves in a tomb. We shall have arisen before the burial takes place. But only those with spiritual vision will be able to witness our resurrection.

You will be well on the road to achieving this spiritual perception, if you accept the fact that even when you are sitting face to face looking at a person and talking with him, you cannot see him. All that you can see is his body, his form; but you cannot see him, because he is way back of his eyes, looking out at you. Furthermore, he cannot see you, because you, also, are back of your eyes, looking out at him. You may be assured of this: If your body were lying on the floor, lifeless, you would still be there looking out at him because this "you" is not encased in a frame. The "you" of you is as external to your body as I *am*, and as I *am* is God.

We are not form, nor are we in a form: The real identity of us animates our form. If the form were destroyed, we would immediately animate another one because that which is I can raise up a new temple three days from now, three hours from now, three minutes from now. There is no such thing as death for any individual. That which we call the death of the form is an experience that comes to us only because of a universal acceptance of birth, maturity, and death. As a matter of fact, our body does die; that is, our *concept* of body has died many times since we were born. There probably is not a drop of blood in us at this moment that was in us a year or two ago or a hair of our head that we had a few years ago.

Every part of us is being built and rebuilt, is dying and being reborn, just like the parts of a tree. The form of a tree is continually dying, but the life of the tree is continually raising up a new form. Every tree has a new form in its cycle of time. So do we have a new body—a new concept of body—whether it is every year, as some physicians say, or every three years as others say. There is no doubt but that many parts of this form, called the body, are dying moment by moment. Some of them, such as the nails or hair, we deliberately remove. Yet because the body dies and is renewed minute by minute we are not even aware of this dying process or of the rebirthing of the body.

We could go on unto eternity watching our body die every year or two, and new blood, new skin, new bones, and new flesh being formed, and never experience the death process or what we term passing on; but when that day of living indefinitely in *this* life-experience comes, it will of necessity bring with it the realization that there is no such thing as old age. Simply living more years and carrying around a weak, infirm body for someone else to bathe, feed, or support is not proving immortality.

Transition is not a physical thing. Transition is an act of consciousness which appears physically. To each of us there comes a time to cease being human beings, to cease living our human lives. That does not mean that we must die; it does not mean that we must pass on to attain our spiritual estate. There are those here who have passed from living a human life and are now living a spiritual life on earth, although, if you were to see them, you might not be aware of the transition they have undergone because their outward appearance is not unlike our own. But that is only the appearance: Actually, they have attained their Christhood.

The Master was an example of a human being who made the transition in consciousness while still living on earth. If you had seen the Master, you would undoubtedly have been one of those who said, "That is our neighbor,

Mary's son," or "That is our neighbor, the carpenter." But if you were of Peter's state of consciousness, you would have known that you were not looking at a carpenter, but at the Christ. To anyone who asked who this man was, you would have responded: "This is not a carpenter; this is the Christ, the Son of God. He has already made the transition and is now living a Christ-life instead of a human life." If this had not been true, Jesus could not have made the demonstration of appearing to the five hundred who witnessed him after the Crucifixion. It was because He, himself, was no longer of the "grave" state of consciousness that He could make himself visible to those who were likewise above the "grave" state of consciousness.

To every man and woman in this present age and in the foreseeable future—even to those who have made the transition to a spiritual state of consciousness—there will probably be a transition from earthly sight. The world may call it death or passing on, but it will not come as a result of old age, disease or accident. Those people who have made this spiritual transition will not experience the torture of endless years of disease, the tragedy of accidents, nor the infirmities of old age, but will walk on to their next experience quickly and painlessly. I am convinced that the day will come when we, in the world, will continue endlessly visible to each other, never aging past the point of maturity. We shall stand forth in the fullness of our realized Christhood, maintaining the full vigour of maturity throughout all time.

———————

Joel S. Goldsmith: Twentieth-century American mystic and spiritual leader whose more than thirty books on spirituality, metaphysics, and mysticism are cherished all over the world and have been a source of inspiration and help to millions.

13

"CARDIAC ARREST REMEMBERED"

(From *The Canadian Medical Association Journal,* May 1971)

R. L. MacMillan, M.D., F.R.C.P. and K. W. G. Brown, M.D., F.R.C.P.

The Tenant

This body is my house—it is not I.
Herein I sojourn till, in some far sky,
I lease a fairer dwelling, built to last.
Till all the carpentry of time is past.
This body is my house—it is not I.
Triumphant in this faith I live, and die.

—Frederick L. Knowles

A sixty-eight-year-old man who previously had suffered no symptoms of coronary artery disease awoke with aching pain in the left arm. Squeezing retrosternal pain developed several hours later and persisted until his admission to the hospital in the late afternoon. He was transferred without delay to the coronary unit, where his general condition was found to be satisfactory. Blood pressure was 126/78, heart sounds were normal, and there were no signs of cardiac failure. A 12-lead electrocardiogram was normal. The heart rhythm was monitored continuously and only an occasional ventricular premature beat was seen that followed the T wave by a comfortable distance. Ten hours after admission, the chest pain became worse and the patient was given 50 mg. of meperidine. Suddenly a ventricular premature beat fell on a T wave, causing ventricular fibrillation. One of the coronary unit nurses recognized the cardiac arrest and immediately defibrillated the patient. After this there were no further serious arrhythmias, and convalescence was uneventful apart from an episode of pulmonary infarction. The ECG was normal the morning after defibrillation, and it was not until the tenth day that changes of anterior subendocardial infarction became evident. Changes in SGOT and CPK levels, however, were diagnostic of recent myocardial infarction from the first day in hospital. The patient remembered in detail the events surrounding his cardiac arrest, and the following account is his own vivid description of his experience. (The right leg mentioned was badly scarred from osteomyelitis suffered in childhood.)

"As I promised, I am setting down my experiences as I remember them when I had the cardiac arrest last May.

"I find it hard to describe certain parts—I do not have words to express how vivid the experience was. The main thing that stands out is the clarity of my thoughts during the episode. They were almost exactly as I have written them and in retrospect it seems that they are fixed in my memory—more so than other things that have happened to me. It seemed at times that I was having a 'dual' sensation—actually experiencing certain things yet at the same time 'seeing' myself during these experiences.

"I had been admitted into the Intensive Care ward in the early evening. I remember looking at my wristwatch and it appeared to be a few minutes before four A.M. I was lying flat on my back because of the intravenous tubes and the wires to the recording machine. Just then I gave a very, very deep sigh and my head flopped over to the right. I thought 'Why did my head flop over?—I didn't move it—I must be going to sleep.' This was apparently my last conscious thought.

"Then I am looking at my own body from the waist up, face to face (as though through a mirror in which I appear to be in the lower left corner). Almost immediately I saw myself leave my body, coming out through my head and shoulders (I did not see my lower limbs). The 'body' leaving me was not exactly in vapor form, yet it seemed to expand very slightly once it was clear of me. It was somewhat transparent, for I could see my other 'body' through it. Watching this I thought, 'So this is what happens when you die' (although no thought of being dead presented itself to me).

"Suddenly I am sitting on a very small object traveling at great speed, out and up into a dull blue-gray sky, at a 45-degree angle. I thought 'It's lonely out here.—Where am I going to end up?—This is one journey I must take alone.'

"Down below to my left I saw a pure white cloudlike substance also moving up on the line that would intersect my course. Somehow I was able to go down and take a look at it. It was perfectly rectangular in shape (about the same proportions as a regular building brick), but full of holes (like a sponge). Two thoughts came to me: 'What will happen to me when it engulfs me?' and 'You don't have to worry; it has all happened before and everything will be taken care of.' I have no recollection of the shape catching up with me.

"My next sensation was of floating in a bright, pale yellow light—a very delightful feeling. Although I was not conscious of having any lower limbs, I felt something being torn off the scars of my right leg, as if a large piece of adhesive tape had been taken off. I thought 'They have always said your body is made whole out here. I wonder if my scars are gone,' but though I tried I could not seem to locate my legs. I continued to float, enjoying the most beautiful tranquil sensation. I had never experienced such a delightful sensation and have no words to describe it.

"Then there were sledge-hammer blows to my left side. They created no actual pain, but jarred me so much that I had difficulty in retaining my balance (on whatever I was sitting). After a number of these blows, I began to count them and when I got to six I said (aloud I think), 'What the . . . are you doing to me?' and opened my eyes.

"Immediately I was in control of all my faculties and recognized the doctors and nurses around me. I asked the head nurse at the foot of my bed, 'What's happening?' and she replied that I'd had a bad turn. I then asked who had been kicking me, and a doctor pointed to a nurse on my left, remarking that she really had to 'thump' me hard and that I would be black and blue on my left side the next day (I don't think I was).

"Just a few comments as I think over what happened to me. I wonder if the bright yellow surroundings could have been caused by someone looking into my eyes with a bright light?

"I have read about heart transplants where it is claimed the brain dies before the heart stops. In my case, my brain must have been working after my heart stopped beating for me to experience these sensations.

"If death comes to a heart patient in this manner, no one has cause to worry about it. I felt no pain (other than what I had when I entered the hospital), and while it was a peculiar experience it was not unpleasant. The floating part of my sensation was so strangely beautiful that I said to a doctor later that night, 'If I go out again, don't bring me back—it's so beautiful out there,' and at that time I meant it."

It is unusual for patients to remember the events surrounding cardiac arrest. More often there is a period of amnesia of several hours' duration before and after the event. This description is extremely interesting. The patient saw himself leaving his body and was able to observe it "face to face." This could be the concept of the soul leaving the body which is found in many religions. The delightful feeling of floating in space and the tranquillity, the yellow light, the rectangular shape with holes in it, associated with the wish of not wanting to be brought back again, may provide comfort and reassurance to patients suffering from coronary artery disease as well as to their relatives.

"Cardiac Arrest Remembered"

This article appeared in The Canadian Medical Association Journal *in May of 1971, and created quite a stir in the medical community, who had not at that time recognized near-death experiences as a legitimate phenomenon. Dr. MacMillan currently lives in Maple, Ontario. Dr. Brown passed away in 1983.*

14

"THE HEREAFTER"

(From *And the Scroll Opened*)

George M. Lamsa

*The soul of man is immortal,
and its future is the future
of a thing whose growth and
splendor has no limit.*

—"The Idyll of the White Lotus"

And it came to pass as the man of God finished speaking on the unknown, he started to explain the hereafter. And he opened his mouth and with a brief sigh, as though he was reluctant to speak on such a subject, he said:

"The thoughts of the hereafter have wearied my soul and caused my sleep to flee. I wandered in this valley and on the high mountains and prayed in solitude in quest of wisdom to know the hereafter. Day and night in my meditation the weight of time and the fear of the unknown and the hereafter have laid heavy upon me.

"In truth, I say unto you, for everything there is an open path and a well-marked exit; and to every riddle there is an answer. Nature declares the glory of God and reveals the secrets of His handiwork. All creations return by the same way that they come and enter by the same gate they left. All creatures bravely and silently come and silently go with no fear or thought of tomorrow and no question about the hereafter. Like the green and tender grass they come and like the dry stubble they go.

"The water slowly and patiently finds its way to its source, the sea. The dust turns into more dust so that the magic touch of the Great Potter's fingers may fashion other vessels. All natural things know that their span of life is like a weaver's web that is cut off when it is finished; and like wayfarers, they are mindful of their departure. The plants store the rays of the sun for the time being and turn them into food, and then let them decay and return to the sun again. From whence they come, thither they go."

He paused, as if gathering his thoughts, and then he spoke again and said, "As the shadows were lengthening and the day darkening and the time of my departure from

137

this temporal life was nigh, the thought of death and the fear of the hereafter haunted me, not so much because of the fear of dying, but because I dreaded the unknown and the life hereafter. I was ready to leave the known and blindly cross the turbulent sea in a ship without a rudder and with no haven in view. And I prayed that the fear which had shut the doors of my vision might be removed, but I found that the more I meditated on the hereafter, the more the dread in my heart increased, and my vision became obscured. Then said I to myself, 'Would that I had been born blind so that I might not have seen the light of the sun and the beauty of this life, and so that the thoughts of the hereafter might not have laid so heavy upon me.'

"Yet in truth, it is only a thin curtain, spun by the fingers of nature and woven on the mysterious loom of time, which hides the known from the unknown, separates the now from the hereafter, the blossom from the fruit, and the sower from the reaper. You have no remembrance of the place from which you came, neither of the day when you first saw the light. Aye, you left the dark and the unknown and opened your eyes unto the known, and you were received like the calm water of a long meandering stream when it reaches its destination, the sea. It knows nothing of its source but calmly merges with the water from which it came, and from which it will emerge again. You came naked and devoid of knowledge and naked and full of knowledge shall you return.

"During your sojourn in this world, you have seen that nature has a single pattern; yea, only one and not two or three. You have learned that the gods of nature have perfect scales and balances, and a single and straight measuring rod for all creations. Now, on this uncertain journey, you will see how the wise and the prudent become speechless, and how the prophet and the seer are helpless in the face of the thought of eternity.

"The Hereafter"

"Now, my brethren and my kinsmen, incline your ear and hearken unto me. In truth, all other creations take this final journey of life bravely, without thought or fear of the life hereafter, and they drink from life's cup like valiant men when they march into the battle with faith and confidence in victory.

"Does the tender and colorful rose know where the wind and storm will hurl its dry petals, or where the breeze will carry its precious scent? Yea, they come quietly and they go quietly, praising the God of Life who adorns them with beauty and glory and then strips them naked and sends them away empty. Aye, they still live secure in the seed of their kind, which they tenderly had nourished, and that will continue to grow and grace the earth to the end of time. And they are mindful that the same gentle and formless hands that planted them have cut them off and will plant them again."

And it came to pass, after a few minutes of silence he spoke again and said, "In vain is your anxiety about the life hereafter. There is an end to man's mortal mind, a limit to his imagination. Oh man, the door of the hereafter is hidden from your eyes, and your journey is on a trackless road with no footprints on the ground nor guideposts to point the way. The reclining shadows of death and the hereafter, your eyes shall never behold; nor can your mortal mind encompass the width of the universe and the heights of the heaven. Can a drop of dew in a desert reveal the vastness of the ocean? Can a man empty a sea with a spoon?"

Then he spoke again and said, "On my arrival at the crossing line which separates the life here from the life hereafter, I was impatient to cross before the messenger of death delivered his dreaded summons. Bravely I drew near the border line trying to get a glimpse of the hereafter, and lo, suddenly a strange man with a fierce countenance appeared before me, and cried with a loud voice and said, 'Do not attempt to cross the line, your turn has not yet come, the weight of time is still upon you.' And I looked, and lo, the strange figure was standing between the light and the darkness, between the known and the hereafter. His apparel was half white and half dark; one of his feet was over the white line and the other over the dark line.

"After I had fearfully observed the strange phenomenon, I said to him, trembling, 'Who are you, my lord?' and he answered, 'I do not know who I am. All I know is that some pilgrims call me life, and others call me death. You can see, I stand with one foot in the light and the other foot in darkness.'

"Then I besought him to tell me what was beyond the dark line, and where was the hereafter. In bewilderment he answered, 'I do not know what kind of life is beyond the dark line for I have never crossed these lines. I have been standing where you see me stand before the earth started to revolve around the sun; yea, before the first shafts of light fell upon it, I was standing here to light the candles that are held in the hands of the myriads of wayfarers who cross the dark line into the light, and to put out the candles of those who cross the white line into the dark.'

"Then I said to him, 'Oh guardian of life and death, I beseech you, tell me where all of these people come from and whither they go.' And he replied, 'This is a secret hidden in a sealed scroll which no one can open, yea, not even the prophets and seers, but only the Lord of Life Himself, who is also the Lord of Death and the Hereafter.'

"And when I awoke I found that it was a revelation. Soon my long-awaited summons came and I was happy to depart.

"Now in truth, I say unto you, in my quest for the life hereafter, I have found that this mortal life is a replica of the life hereafter. Death is nothing but an eternal change, an infinity, and the life hereafter begins right now. The little acorn which once was held and nourished by the tender bough, is buried in the ground and becomes a large oak tree to bear more acorns on its boughs.

"Verily, I say unto you, even after you have crossed the white line into the dark and the dreaded unknown, you will see the light of His countenance penetrating the grave, and hear the small voice even in the solitude of the earth. Aye, it was in the grim silence and thick darkness that your body was conceived and fashioned and in which the immortal and the mortal joined hands to dance in a timeless space. Out of a sunless and starless universe you emerged and in the stillness of time you shall depart carrying your burning candle in your hand. For out of the darkness comes forth light, and out of the light, immortality.

"In truth, life is like a candle from which myriads of candles are lighted. And, even though all light appears the same, there is a difference, for no two candles are alike. All the grains of sand are similar, but no two are alike. Consider the flowers of the field: Some of them are graced with beauty and majesty, worthy to be placed on the king's table. But some, even though they are clothed with glorious colors, are thorny. Yet, they are still cultivated by the same Gardener and nourished by the same hidden forces and watered by the same stream.

"In death and in life man's identity is eternal. Consider the precious diamonds: They all have brilliant colors, but are diverse, one from another. Aye, there are not two leaves on a tree which are alike, neither do two flakes of snow contain the same design. Verily, I say unto you, every man is an eternal flower with a different scent in the Great Garden of the God of Life.

"Life cannot be weighed on scales, nor separated into forms or degrees, for life is measureless, embracing all, and is manifested in diverse forms and degrees. Life was never created, nor will it die. In truth, life is the eternal wine made from the vine planted by the fingers of God to be drunk by angels and men, by mortals and immortals, by the saints and the sinners. And, being so great and precious, it is hidden even from the eyes of the angels.

"Verily, I say unto you, the secret of the hereafter is buried in its own seed. Yea, the riddle is beyond the comprehension of the wise and the prudent. The Life hereafter is the dream of today fulfilled tomorrow, and man, being a spark of life, cannot explain the secret of life. How can a vessel understand the potter, its maker, or describe the touch of his gentle fingers? How can the leaves explain the intricate design the roots have woven in the dark and hidden chambers of the ground? Only life can disclose its secret. Only the sea can feel the weight of the water which it contains, and only the wings can measure the thinness of the air.

"Aye, the hereafter is hidden in the bygone yesterday, and the secret of today in the unborn tomorrow, and the riddle of eternity is hidden in the beginning. Life lives with those who know how to live and dies with those who know how to die, and is born with those who are born, and sleeps with those who sleep in the dust, to raise them again to life.

"The Cup of Life is full and running over; its suns never set, its dawns never darken, and its horizons are limitless."

George M. Lamsa (1892–1958): Author and founder of Christian Jewish Mohammedans Society, whose purpose was to bring an understanding between the sects.

142

15

LIFE AND IMMORTALITY
TO LIGHT

Jess E. Weiss

Death is nothing but an Eternal change, an Infinity, and the Life hereafter begins right now.

—Jess E. Weiss

Life beyond this human experience transcends human consciousness and is called by many names: Fourth dimensional, Cosmic, Spiritual, Mystical, or the *I AM* consciousness. From the very beginning of creation, mankind has sought an answer to the question: Is there continuity of life after death?

Some of the most vivid descriptions of a life after death, and a foretaste of a life beyond this human experience, come from the voices, including the voices of children, of those who have been called back from the brink of death. They say that as they moved toward death they seemed to enter a cosmic dimension, another state of conscious being where time and space and corporeal sense were absent:

They felt no pain or suffering during the experience.
In fact, they recalled a feeling of tranquillity and peace.
They had a panoramic view of their entire lives.
They felt the presence of loved ones who had died earlier.
They were in the presence of an undefined radiant Light.
They went through a tunnel and upon their return to human life-form, death was no longer the enemy to fear.
*They were very certain afterward that life goes on without interruption after the body dies.**

*From *Overcoming the Fear of Death and Dying, A Sense of Life that Knows No Death,* by Jess E. Weiss, 1991. An edition in Braille, 1993.

THE VESTIBULE

The near-death experience is nothing new. The Bible is quite descriptive in its account of similar occurrences centuries ago. Elijah the prophet restored life to the dead son of the widow of Zarephath. The seer Elisha brought back to life the dead child of the woman from Shunem. Jesus startled all of Galilee with the raising of the widow's son in the city of Nain. Later, He raised from the dead the twelve-year-old daughter of Jairus, a leader of a Jewish synagogue. On the Mount of Transfiguration (transcending human consciousness), with three of His disciples, Jesus talked with Moses and Elias, Hebrew prophets who were supposed to have died centuries before. No doubt Jesus' greatest miracles were the raising of Lazarus from his grave after he had been dead for four days, and His own final act of raising himself out of His tomb on the third day. Jesus' victory over death and His triumph over the "last enemy" assures us that we, too, will live after the death of our bodies.

The apostle Peter (about 40 A.D.) emulated Jesus' victory when he brought back to life a disciple named Dorcas, a woman much-loved and known for her "good works and almsdeeds." And the converted Pharisee Paul (54–58 A.D.) embraced a young man named Eutychus, who in a deep sleep had fallen down from the third loft as Paul was preaching late, "was taken up dead" and restored to life.

The fear of death is deeply rooted. The harder one clings to life, the more terrifying death becomes. Most human beings repress their fear of death and live as though they are "immortal mortals" and will never die. They deny that which is as much a part of human life as birth. Even the *American Medical Journal* in its September, 1968 issue acknowledges: "By virtue of its uniformity, universality, and inevitability, death is perhaps the most normal of all physiological states."

Does life begin at a point called birth and end at another called death? Or do we believe that life begins for us here and that we can look forward to immortality hereafter? How can we as human beings hope to awaken to our innate nature *"the immortal Self at one with God,"* which is infinite, invisible, intangible, immutable, but unknowable to human sense? It all begins when one reaches a point in life, through fear of losing this life, by hopelessness, helplessness, terminal illness, or adulthood coming to an end, when one asks: *Is this all? Is this transient, mortal sense of existence all there is? Or is earth a place of preparation for understanding and awakening to another life after death?*

Eternal life, immortality, is the gift of God. This gift was given to each of us at the time we were created—from the very beginning. As long as we maintain our identity in a conscious sense of undyingness, then a sense of deathlessness operates within us and immortality is alive. The pattern or common denominator of the near-death experiences gives us objective evidence of what to expect when we die.

The body is the abode of mortality and consciousness is the abode of immortality; but birth does not separate us from immortality and death cannot take it away.

The belief in death as terminal is a godless vestibule to unbeing, nothingness. If we who were created in God's "image and likeness" are born and eventually terminated, then cannot God die also? They who question the existence of God also question the existence of life after death. If God, *"The I AM that I AM,"* is immortal, and if Jesus *"His Shepherd"* is immortal, then so is God's creation. The vital question is: How can we become alive to the *consciousness* of immortality and dead to the mind's sense of mortality even while we reside in this mutable, external garment called body?

Deathlessness lies hidden in the consciousness of every human being. The purpose of this human life, which has been called "a Parenthesis in Eternity," is to discover birthlessness and deathlessness of one's infinite being. We progress in the unfolding of the *infinite* nature of consciousness while in the body, so our progression after death even as before death is the measure of knowing "deathlessness." Our "Shepherd," Jesus the Christ, abolished the sense of death as reality, and brought life and immortality to light.

There is a modern story of two men on a dais before a large religious gathering who were asked to repeat the Twenty-Third Psalm: "The Lord *is* my *Shepherd*." The first was a young man with a glorious, melodious, resonating voice. When he finished, the audience gave him a standing ovation. Then the other got up, a very old man, and he spoke in a slow, soft, hesitatingly cracked voice, anything but grandiloquent. When he finished, there wasn't a sound. Within a few moments, the young man got up again and said: "Do you know what the difference was between the two of us? . . . I knew the Psalm . . . but he knew the *Shepherd*."

As the experiences of the men and women in this book reveal, immortality is *Now*. It has no past and no future . . . no beginning and no ending. Man does not die out of mortality into immortality, because the soul of man is as immortal as God is. It is a "within" awareness. Immortality and God are synonymous terms, and when we know God *within*, we know undyingness, a life after the mortal concept of death. The destruction of death as *"the last enemy"* to be overcome is our spiritual obligation. Right here. Right now. Death is an experience of the spiritless unawakened human mind, the mind that tells us we are physical, mortal, finite, terminal. The belief in death as terminal implies an end to any further God-creative process.

Death loses its sting, the grave its victory, when we realize the Eternity of our own being. David the Psalmist sang, "Yea, *though* I walk *through* the valley of the shadow of death, I will fear no evil: for Thou *art* with me. . . ." (Ps. 23:4.) Those who fear death less can live a more purposeful life. *"The last enemy* that shall be destroyed is *death"* (I Cor. 15–26): That was the apostle Paul's mystical revelation. By this he meant that our earthly concept of body, the one we have now that dies, *must* sooner or later be transformed into that heavenly body that cannot perish but will live forever. Then are the scriptures fulfilled: *"Death is swallowed up in victory."* (I Cor. 15:54.)

The spiritually awakened know they do not have to become immortal—they know they already are. Life to them is a mystical journey beyond words and thoughts— beyond humanism. During the past centuries countless mystics have entertained this higher form of consciousness than that possessed by the ordinary man. Death is *"conquered"* by having a concept of body as an outward garment consciously being undressed and spiritually redressed for renewal. Jesus was spiritually unchanged by the experience called death, and even so are we, here as well as hereafter. This illumined or enlightened mystical state of consciousness places the individual on a new plane of existence in which he enjoys a state of moral exaltation, an indescribable feeling of elevation; a sense of immortality; a sense of being in the world but not of it. Through mysticism a person achieves a sense not that he shall have these, but an awareness that he has them already . . . that he brought them with him.

Unawakened mortals subliminally "put on" immortality only as their conscious sense of mortality becomes less important. Therefore, the less one is enamored with temporary earth-life, the easier it is to approach immortal God-life. Paul admonishes us, "Set your affection on things above, not on things on the earth." (Col. 3:2.)

To acquire this mystical awakening, therefore, man has to make spirituality the primary objective of everyday life, and the absolute requirement for a genuine spiritual life is to do what Paul did: *"Die daily"* (I Cor. 15:31), meaning one must die to one level of consciousness and be reborn in a higher one, above words and thoughts, above even metaphysics, or the letter of truth into the mystical consciousness of truth, where the Infinite Invisible is, where the lost spiritual years are restored, and where the last enemy—"death"—is overcome, and the imprisoned splendor—immortality—is revealed.

The search for immortality is a search for life after death and it is a mystical journey intent upon knowing God aright, without a road map, without a compass, sometimes with a teacher . . . sometimes without. Immortality is not a religion but a mystical revelation and a rescue from mortality. To live with a sense of immortal Sonship is the elixir of life; it dissolves the fear of death and dying. We are then a part of something greater than ourselves. It is that *Something* beyond form, but which appears as form. To live solely as a human being whose life begins and will sooner or later end, is to live in darkness without hope and without Light. We have no hope beyond the grave unless *Something* greater than ourselves can revive us from the belief and fear of death.

Life seems intelligible only as the avenue and *vestibule*

Life and Immortality to Light

for *another* life. The willingness to believe that life continues after death *is* the beginning of the realization that Infinite *Being* is our divine life. The desire to believe *is* the grain of mustard seed that prepares the way for *"the Vestibule"* experience, which comes to all in its own good way and in its own good time.

I AM

Do not stand by my grave and weep;
I AM not there. I do not sleep.
I AM a thousand winds that blow,
I AM a diamond glint of snow.
I AM the sunlight on ripened grain,
I AM the gentle autumn rain.
When you awake in the morning hush,
I AM the swift uplifting rush
Of quiet birds in circling flight.
I AM the soft starshine of night.
Do not stand by my grave and cry;
I AM not there . . . I did not die.

This world is like
a vestibule before
the World to Come;
prepare thyself in the
vestibule that thou
mayest enter into the Hall. . . .

DiMaggio/Kalish © 1996

LaVergne, TN USA
11 December 2009
166804LV00001B/152/A